Separate Account Bank-Owned Life Insurance

The Theory and Practice

Tom Wamberg, CLU

The information and data in this publication were obtained from sources considered reliable. Their accuracy or completeness is not guaranteed, and the giving of the same is not deemed an offer or solicitation on our part with respect to the sale or purchase of any securities mentioned herein. This publication is not to be used as a substitute for any reports distributed by your variable insurance carrier.

This publication is designed to provide accurate and authoritative information about the subject covered. While every precaution has been taken in the preparation of this material, The American College assumes no liability for damages resulting from the use of the information contained in this publication. The American College is not engaged in rendering legal, accounting, or other professional advice. If legal or other expert advice is required, the services of an appropriate professional should be sought.

Library of Congress Control Number: 2006933244
ISBN 1932819398

Printed in the United States of America

The American College's Monograph Series

For several years, we have felt the need for a way to provide special ideas, proposals, and concepts to our students, our alumni, and to friends of The College.

The publications in this ongoing Monograph Series bring you education from leading financial advisors, an excellent supplement to the scholarly knowledge embedded in our various books, online courses, and tools.

Laurence Barton, PhD
President and Chief Executive Officer

Walt Woerheide, PhD, CFP
Vice President of Academics and Dean

TABLE OF CONTENTS

About The Author

Tom Wamberg, CLU, is the Chairman and Chief Executive Officer of Clark Consulting, (NYSE: CLK), the creators of BOLI and the largest seller and administrator of Bank-Owned Life Insurance. The company currently serves 2,100 banking clients. Mr. Wamberg's office is located in North Barrington, Illinois, where the company designs, implements and administers sophisticated life insurance plans for banks and commercial corporations. In addition, Clark owns Pearl Meyer & Partners, an executive compensation firm, the Federal Policy Group, a federal tax specialist, and the Healthcare Group, which offers total compensation and benefits services to Healthcare clients.

The author's professional memberships include the American Compensation Association, American Society of Pension Actuaries, Society of Financial Service Professionals, and the Young Presidents' Organization. Tom Wamberg has also served as the President of the International Forum, the President of the Association for Advanced Life Underwriting, and is on the board of Trustees of the Cleveland Clinic and SIFE. He is also the author of *The Theory and Practice of Bank Owned Life Insurance*, 1995.

FOREWORD

For decades, there were very few product variables in the insurance industry. Most salespersons had one or two product lines to sell. They worked for one company and were "captive." Consumers had few choices. What everyone agreed on, however, was that the founder of The American College, Dr. Solomon S. Huebner, completely captured the essence of what our profession is about when he advanced the importance of "human life value."

Employers understand human life value, and this is one of the reasons they often encourage their employees to purchase life insurance. Investors do as well, which leads to the increasing attention to corporate-owned and bank-owned life insurance.

Today, with several dozens of variations of products available, the importance of understanding the dynamics of each of these product categories can help you be more informed and, concurrently, advance the opportunity you have to help your clients. Thus, this thought-provoking and timely work by one of the leaders of our industry, Tom Wamberg, is especially compelling. Rather than written by a theorist, it has been written by an industry champion who understands the practical dimensions of how these alternative products are presented in the marketplace.

The American College is continually adapting to a vibrant financial services marketplace. I know you will find that this work makes an important contribution to our profession.

Larry Barton, PhD
President and Chief Executive Officer
Professor of Management
The American College

ACKNOWLEDGMENTS

This book could not have been produced without the help of many talented professionals at Clark Consulting who were instrumental in rigorously writing, reviewing and editing sections that pertain to their specialties within our company.

Bruce D. Bengston
Senior Vice President
Actuary

Richard C. Callister
Senior Managing Director
Senior Vice President

Timothy L. Hanford
Director

Kenneth J. Kies
Managing Director

Kurt Laning
Chief Actuary

Scott Richardson
Senior Consultant

Tom Wamberg, CLU
Barrington Hills, IL
August 2006

Introduction

Bank-Owned Life Insurance (BOLI) has become a very popular tool for banks to finance the cost of their employee benefit liabilities. Introduced in 1983, BOLI today is owned by more than 3,000 banks.

This book discusses how BOLI works and the reasons why banks increasingly use this product. In addition, it helps readers find their way through the maze of decisions that have to be made when purchasing a BOLI plan.

Bank-Owned Life Insurance presents a unique financial opportunity. *Separate Account Bank-Owned Life Insurance: The Theory and Practice,* enables readers and bankers to understand the separate account BOLI product in detail. This knowledge will allow the readers to become more sophisticated in their understanding of Separate Account Bank-Owned Life Insurance.

Life Insurance Product Selection

The main thrust of this book is to review the various life insurance products that are available to banks. In the life insurance world, a life insurance policy is called a product.

In the early years of BOLI, the only product available was called general account. With the passage of time and the development of new financial instruments, particularly the stable value rider, which is discussed in Chapter 5, Separate Account Life Insurance, more banks became buyers of separate account products.

It is expected the Separate Account Product will become the predominant product of choice for all but the smallest banks.

There has never been a book written that covers the subject matter at hand. Therefore, *Separate Account Bank-Owned Life Insurance: The Theory and Practice* will delve deeply into the working of all facets of separate account life insurance products.

CHAPTER 1
An Overview Of Bank-Owned Life Insurance

Since 1983, banks have successfully profited with Bank-Owned Life Insurance (BOLI), and in the past decade the product has gained wide acceptance within the banking community as a sound financial strategy. BOLI is insurance owned by the bank. The bank is also the beneficiary of the policies. Most banks have found that BOLI can provide after-tax returns 200 to 300 basis points higher than traditional bank investments with low risk.

The main reason banks use Bank-Owned Life Insurance is to finance the cost of employee benefit plans. These expenses are a major overhead component for most banks. Any financing tool which can lower or stabilize this cost is of great value.

Recent studies have suggested that benefit plan expenses will continue to increase at a much faster pace than the rate of increase in banks' interest income. Any plan that can control this increase makes good financial sense. BOLI is the most powerful tool available to help banks with this problem.

Banks gain two main advantages from using BOLI: the plan's yield is greater than that available from alternative investments, and the long-term nature of the program corresponds with the extended time horizon of benefit plan expenses.

HOW BOLI WORKS

A bank purchases life insurance covering a group of employees, not to exceed the top 35 percent of employees ranked by compensation. Banks may not simply purchase BOLI as an investment. The amount of coverage must conform with the bank's allowable benefit liabilities. (Bank regulatory issues are discussed in detail in Chapter 10.)

Once the number of employees to be insured has been selected and the size of the premium has been determined, the policies are issued to the bank. Most BOLI plans require only a one-time premium deposit.[1] The bank pays the premium and owns the entire cash value of the policies. The bank is also the beneficiary of the life insurance proceeds. Employees generally do not receive any of the insurance

[1] This is called "single premium life insurance" and is a modified endowment contract. Modified endowment contracts are explained in Chapter 4.

proceeds directly, nor do they pay any of the premium. The coverage is entirely separate from other insurance coverage provided by the bank, such as group term insurance.

BOLI is not a new benefit for employees. It simply helps the bank pay for the benefits currently provided. Employees have reacted favorably to BOLI plans when they understand that BOLI allows their employer to finance its benefit plan obligations without requiring any payments from employees.

From a financial perspective, BOLI provides a bank with a high tax-free yield. The bank can pay premiums with funds derived from selling portfolio investments with lower tax-adjusted yields, such as U.S. Treasury securities and corporate bonds. (Chapter 4 illustrates how the yields from BOLI compare to these alternatives.)

Numerous studies demonstrate the relative advantages of BOLI measured over a period of decades. These analyses illustrate how insurance carriers can pass on competitive, tax-favored yields to banks.

A BOLI plan generates additional income as early as the first year it is put into effect and it continues producing additional income each year it is in force. The income comes from two sources: the growth of the asset (the cash value) and from the payment of death benefits to the bank when employees die.

From an accounting point of view, BOLI is subject to "FASB Technical Bulletin 85-4" (see Appendix B). This advisory was issued in 1985 in response to a request from the life insurance industry for an accounting standard covering life insurance owned by a corporation. Unlike accounting for some other financial instruments, the accounting treatment for BOLI is straightforward and noncontroversial.

> BOLI plans have been promoted as a solution to the FAS 106 problem which requires a corporation to accrue for the cost of post-employment benefits other than pensions. BOLI is an acceptable funding device, but only if placed in a 501 (c) (9) trust, commonly called a voluntary employee benefit association (VEBA).
>
> To qualify as a funded asset, BOLI has to be placed in the VEBA, and must follow all VEBA trust rules which are, in turn, governed by the federal Employee Retirement Income Security ACT (ERISA). The main deterrent to placing the BOLI in a VEBA trust is that proceeds must be dedicated exclusively to funding employee benefit plans. If the funds flow back to the corporation, they become taxable. To avoid this, most banks have elected to purchase BOLI at the bank level, where it is exempt from the requirement that policies be placed in a trust.

Once the decision to purchase BOLI is made, the next step is to choose a life insurance carrier that has an acceptable performance record and financial credit rating. (Carrier selection is covered in Chapter 6.)

LEGAL ISSUES

A number of legal issues must be addressed in designing a BOLI plan. Life insurance regulations require that policies be filed and approved in the state of domicile of the bank. A multi-state banking company must adhere to the insurance laws of the state where its corporate headquarters is located. State insurance laws are generally consistent, but the laws in the state of the bank's main location govern. In addition, a BOLI plan must follow the insurable interest laws of the host state. Such laws regulate the amount of coverage a bank can buy on any employee.

CONSULTANTS AND ADMINISTRATORS

A final consideration is choosing a consultant to assist in designing and implementing a plan, and an administrator to manage it over its expected life span of more than 40 years.

Naturally, the quality of consultants and administrators plays a large role in determining the ultimate profitability of the plan.

The BOLI design and implementation process is straightforward. However, it can sometimes be clouded by hyperbole and confusion. Any buyer who follows the steps laid out in this book can avoid the pitfalls and will find the BOLI process easy to follow. By taking advantage of the advice contained herein, a buyer will be in a position to maximize the BOLI opportunity.

CHAPTER 2
BOLI AND BENEFIT COSTS

Employee benefits are a significant expense item in bank compensation programs, comprising 20 to 30 percent or more of all compensation costs. Employee compensation is generally the second largest expense item for financial institutions. Only the cost of funds is a greater expense.

Financial organizations, like all businesses, are concerned with the rising cost of employee benefits. BOLI allows them to design a plan that will offset a portion of employee benefit expenses and enhance financial performance. This chapter explains the calculations required to determine a bank's benefit costs and, therefore, the amount of BOLI a bank may buy.

Generally, banks are not allowed to invest in life insurance products. Under specific circumstances, banks may purchase life insurance to offset employee expense obligations. Regulators who oversee the safe and sound management of financial institutions have formulated guidelines for implementing BOLI plans.

The Office of the Comptroller of the Currency (OCC) regulates allowable transactions for nationally chartered banks. The Office of Thrift Supervision (OTS) regulates savings associations. State banking agencies regulate state-chartered banks, which are also under the jurisdiction of the Federal Reserve System or the Federal Deposit Insurance Corporation (FDIC). These four regulatory agencies jointly issued the Interagency Statement on the Purchase and Risk Management of Life Insurance in December 2004. The Interagency Statement limits the amount of life insurance a financial institution may purchase to an amount corresponding with benefit costs. In addition, the amount purchased may not exceed a certain percentage of a bank's capital and legal lending limits.

EMPLOYEE BENEFIT EXPENSES AND BOLI

For virtually every employee, benefits are a significant portion of overall compensation. Human resources managers regularly evaluate competitive practices and products in the marketplace to ensure their programs provide benefits that are meaningful, competitive, reasonable, and cost-efficient. When financial institutions provide benefits for their employees, an obligation is created.

Regulators have recognized the long-term cost of employee benefits by allowing financial institutions to utilize BOLI plans to offset their continuing liability. It is this continuing benefit liability that establishes the maximum limits for BOLI plan purchases by each financial institution. Regulators want to ensure that banks can meet benefit obligations without jeopardizing depositors or shareholders.

The Interagency Statement defines the circumstances under which national banks may own life insurance. The main principle of the Interagency Statement is clear:

> A bank may, therefore, purchase insurance on a group of persons and continue to hold the insurance as long as it has any liability under the associated compensation or benefit plan.

It is a common interpretation of the Interagency Statement that expenses associated with funded benefits are included in determining overall benefit expense obligations. Nonqualified benefit expenses are also included in calculating expense obligations. Employee benefit plans that are typically included in the calculation of expense obligations for BOLI are:

- Post-Retirement Medical
- Life Insurance
- Retirement Plan Expense – Qualified and Nonqualified

Calculating benefit expenses and obligations for BOLI is relatively straightforward. The maximum amount of coverage that may be purchased is determined according to the following procedure:

1. For each employee, the current benefit cost is calculated, and then projected over the employee's working career.
2. The present value of the total employee benefit cost is then calculated for the date of BOLI plan implementation.
3. The total present value benefit cost for all employees is determined. This establishes the BOLI plan maximum limitations.

Since the bank in our example below has 1,000 employees who are in the top 35 percent by compensation, the maximum amount of insurance the bank can hold in its BOLI plan (on a present value basis) is $30,453 times 1,000 employees or $30,453,000. This means the total benefit from the insurance policies cannot exceed a present value of $30,453,000. The limit corresponds to the bank's maximum employee benefit obligation of $30,453,000. Purchasing insurance beyond the benefit obligation is considered an investment and is not allowed.

PRESENT VALUE BENEFIT COST FOR ONE SAMPLE INDIVIDUAL
MALE, AGE 39

Current Annual Cost	Inflation Factor	Future Value of Annual Benefit Cost at Age 65	Present Value of Annual Benefit Costs at 4%
Group Term Life			
$190	5%	$676	$5,826
Pension Costs			
$400	5%	$1,422	$12,265
Post-Retirement Medical			
$320	7%	$1,858	$12,362
	Total Net Present Value Cost		**$30,453**

Individual policies in a BOLI plan do not have to match the level of liability of each covered person. For example, a smaller group of employees can be insured to offset the costs associated with all 1,000 employees. This is called aggregate funding, as opposed to specific funding. In many cases, a bank will only insure its officers, purchasing enough BOLI to offset the benefit costs for all employees. It is more efficient to insure a smaller group of employees and policy administration is simpler.

It is not required that BOLI plan assets be segregated. They may be commingled with other bank assets. Appreciation in BOLI cash value is used to offset the cost of benefit expenses or obligations and is tax-free. Insurance proceeds are also nontaxable income to the bank.

Banks, their consultants, or actuaries use census information for each employee—age, sex, compensation, and other information—to calculate the present value cost of benefit expenses or obligations. In turn, the present value cost of benefit expenses determines the face amount of each policy. Insurance carriers also require adherence to insurable interest rules[1], which are aimed at preventing banks from collecting "profit" when an employee dies.

The concept that banks stand to profit from employee deaths is a frequent misconception about BOLI plans. Except in extraordinary circumstances, such as the death of large numbers of covered employees soon after plan implementation, banks do not profit from the death of any employee in a BOLI plan.

Banks can only purchase life insurance equal to the present value limits of their employee benefit expenses and are not allowed to speculate or over-insure any employee.

Insurance carriers limit the amount of insurance they will place on any single person based on insurable interest. The owner of the policy, a bank, must have an interest in the life of the insured, an employee. In most states, the net death benefits from a policy cannot be greater than the loss to a bank when an employee dies.

Sometimes, when employees die early in a BOLI plan, a bank may appear to profit. But the plan is designed to finance a long-term obligation. In calculating that obligation,

[1] *Insurable Interest:* A bank must have an insurable interest to purchase life insurance on an employee. An explanation of insurable interest is covered in detail, on page 28.

an expected mortality pattern for the total employee group is factored in.

INSURABLE INTEREST—THE GUIDELINES

In order for a bank to insure an employee, it must have an insurable interest.[2] Insurable interest laws in this country were first enacted at the beginning of the 20th century. Centuries ago in England, it was common to take bets or place insurance on the life of a sick person. Bettors would try to predict when a person would die. In the United States, many states passed insurable interest laws outlawing this morbid practice.

From the early part of this century until the mid–1980s, the insurable interest laws were adequate for business practices. However, in the mid–1980s, a number of major companies set up Corporate Owned Life Insurance plans, the first time that large numbers of employees were insured with their employers as beneficiaries.

---

[2] *For more detailed information, please see:*
Greider, Janice E., et al. *Law and Life Insurance Contract.* Homewood, Illinois: Richard D. Irwin, Inc. 1984
Skipper, Harold and Black, Kenneth. *Life and Health Insurance, 13th Edition.* Paramus, New Jersey: Prentice Hall, Inc. 1999

Prior to 1985, most corporations insured only their top executives for the benefit of the company. This concept of key–person insurance is well founded in the law and has been used extensively.

However, when corporations began to insure large groups or all employees, not just key persons, it raised the question of whether they were gambling on the probability of death of their employees, thereby running afoul of insurable interest laws. Of course, they were not really doing so because the basic idea behind buying Corporate Owned Life Insurance is to offset the cost of death, not to make a profit.

The concept of insurable interest holds that a beneficiary, whether a family member or an employer, must have a pecuniary (monetary) loss that corresponds with the amount of life insurance carried on an insured person's life. The potential for a financial loss on one person's death creates an insurable interest for another person or entity that would suffer the loss.

Any individual may potentially be insured by a number of people or entities. For example, family members who are financially dependent on the bread winner have an insurable interest. The bread winner's employer would also suffer a loss if the employee died. Therefore, the employer also has an insurable interest, although the amount may be different.

In employer/employee situations, there are well-established procedures for determining the amount of insurable interest. The first step is to consider the insurable interest laws covering the employer that is buying the coverage. Insurance is under the jurisdiction of the states. Employers with employees in many states will normally be governed by the laws of the state in which they have their corporate headquarters. A number of states have enacted new insurable interest laws.

The amount of coverage that may be purchased is determined by the employer's employee benefit plan expenses, similar to the standard applied in the Interagency Statement.

The Interagency Statement varies from the states' approach in the types of benefits used in determining an allowable transaction. The types of benefits mentioned in the Interagency Statement are:

- Post-retirement medical benefits
- Life insurance benefits
- Nonqualified retirement plan benefits

Most of the states allow a corporation to insure an employee for an amount equal to the present value cost of the corporation's ERISA welfare benefit plans. ERISA welfare benefit plans include all non-retirement benefit programs.

The cost of benefits and the amount of insurance which can be purchased is determined on an *aggregate* basis. This means the total amount of insurance cannot exceed the total amount of benefit costs for all employees. The amount of insurance on any individual employee can be more or less than the cost for that particular employee, as long as the present value gain of the insurance on all employees does not exceed the benefit cost for the overall employee population. This method is known as the welfare benefit projection method.

In states without new insurable interest laws, corporations can insure non-key employees by completing a pecuniary loss calculation. This calculation is somewhat subjective and should be done by a firm that is knowledgeable about insurable interest regulations.

Under a pecuniary loss or pecuniary interest approach, a corporation must define the amount of loss it stands to suffer on the death of an employee. This loss is determined by the cost an employer would incur for benefits when an employee dies, plus any loss of productivity. Most corporations have group term life plans which have an experience rated feature. Under an experience rated plan, a corporation has a premium structure tied to the amount of its claims. For example, assume a typical employee has a salary of $50,000 and a group term life benefit of twice salary, or $100,000. If the employee were to die, the corporation would be charged the amount of the claim plus the carrier's expense margin, normally four percent. Therefore, the company's cost should be $104,000.

In addition, the employer would have other costs associated with the death of the employee, such as hiring and retraining costs. Studies show these costs average from two to 12 times a person's salary. Conservatively, the employer would incur another $100,000 in such costs upon the employee's death.

In addition, there is a factor for salary growth. Normally, a corporation would only insure an employee one time. Therefore, it is reasonable to add another two times salary to cover pay increases.

Total potential costs add up as follows:

Average Employee Salary	$50,000
Employer's Cost at Death	
• Group Term Life (two times salary plus 4% for carrier's expense margin)	104,000
• Hiring & Retraining (two times salary)	100,000
• Survivor Benefits	50,000
• Salary Inflation (two times salary)	100,000
TOTAL =	$ 404,000

Either the employee benefit plan expense method or the pecuniary loss method is useful to satisfy state statutes and insurance carrier requirements. The calculations performed under the Interagency Statement and the insurable interest determination reinforce each other, providing a strong undergirding for BOLI-face amounts.

A few final points: First, a bank only needs an insurable interest in an employee at the time the coverage is written. If the employee leaves, coverage can remain in force. The law recognizes that if insurance were required to be canceled at termination of employment, it would not mature as a death benefit, and would be paid as a cash surrender. If a policy is surrendered, the cash value in excess of premiums is taxable as ordinary income. State laws are designed to avoid forcing employers, or individuals for that matter, to cancel insurance and pay tax. Therefore, coverage is allowed to remain in force until death of the insured. Second, in order to receive favorable federal income tax treatment, the bank cannot insure more than 35 percent of its workforce ranked by compensation.

CHAPTER 3
THE VARIETY OF BOLI PRODUCTS

To those buying insurance, the number of products can seem endless. Choosing the best one is a daunting task. However, armed with an understanding of life insurance, and how various products are built, banks will be able to select the products that best suit their needs.

> Broadly, life insurance products can be categorized as either term or permanent. Term life insurance provides coverage for a limited period of time and develops little or no cash value. In contrast, permanent life insurance provides coverage over the entire lifetime of the insured and generates cash value while the insured is alive. BOLI plans are always permanent life insurance because the cash value growth associated with this insurance is a key source of the earnings offered by the program.

Cash value generated by permanent life insurance represents an asset for an insurance company. To back up that liability, the insurance company sets up a policy reserve. The method for determining the minimum policy reserve is regulated by state insurance departments, although an insurance company may strengthen its reserve position above the minimum at its discretion.

These reserve assets are held either in an insurance company's general account or in one or more separate accounts. Products whose supporting assets reside in an insurance company's general account are called portfolio products. Products whose supporting assets are held in separate accounts are referred to as variable products.

Whether portfolio or variable, a permanent life insurance product comes in one of four basic policy types, or chassis. The difference among them is a matter of mechanics, not value, which is determined by an insurance company's pricing and reflected in the levels of cash value and death benefits provided.

GENERAL ACCOUNT AND SEPARATE ACCOUNT PRODUCTS

Traditionally, insurance companies have sold products that promise fixed-dollar benefit payments when covered events occur, such as the death of insured person. Assets that back these liabilities are held in an insurance company's general account.

Many of today's sophisticated insurance buyers are not satisfied with fixed-dollar benefits. They are keenly aware of the attractive returns available from the securities markets. The bull markets of the 1980s and the early 1990s fed the demand for products that would allow insurance buyers to capture market gains.

Responding to that need, many insurance companies now offer products whose benefit levels vary according to the market value of underlying assets. Insurance companies hold these assets in separate accounts from their general accounts. The products supported by these assets are referred to as separate account products.

General and separate account products also differ in the extent of liability of the insurance company. In addition to the fixed-dollar benefit liabilities, the general account is also charged with the general liabilities of the insurance company. In contrast, assets of separate accounts cannot be charged with liabilities that arise from other company business. Thus, a separate account product provides a BOLI buyer a greater degree of credit risk protection than a general account product.

PRODUCT CHASSIS

Permanent life insurance products are offered in one of four chassis: traditional whole life, interest-sensitive whole life, universal life, and variable life insurance.

TRADITIONAL WHOLE LIFE

Traditional whole life, as its name suggests, is the oldest form of permanent life insurance, and accounted for most permanent life insurance sales until the 1980s. Beginning in the late 1970s, when interest rates were rising rapidly, the insurance industry suffered severe disintermediation by policyowners. To stem this tide, the industry developed products that responded more quickly and more visibly to interest rate movements. These products took the form of either interest-sensitive whole life or universal life.

When a policyowner buys a traditional whole life policy, he or she buys a schedule or guaranteed minimum cash value and death benefits. The guaranteed policy values are calculated based on a four percent interest rate and the 1980 Commissioners Standard Ordinary (CSO) Mortality

Table. An insurance company makes an additional promise—though not a guarantee—to pay any excess profits back to the policyowner in the form of dividends. The sources of excess profits may be:

- Better-than-planned mortality experience
- Better-than-planned investment return
- Better-than-planned expense outlays

Forms of Dividends

An insurance company normally reviews its dividend formula once or twice a year. At each anniversary, the company calculates the dividend payable on the policy based on the prevailing dividend formula. A policyowner may take the dividend in a number of forms:

- Cash
- Paid-up life insurance
- One-year term insurance

Under the paid-up life insurance option, the dividend is used to purchase additional permanent life insurance coverage that requires no further premium payments and permanently increases the policyowner's coverage. With the one-year term insurance option, the dividend is used to purchase coverage that lasts only one year. This represents a temporary increase in coverage greater than that which could be purchased under the paid-up life insurance option.

Non-forfeiture Options

A policyowner must pay the scheduled premium when it is due to keep the traditional whole life policy in force. If the premium is not paid during a grace period of 30 to 60 days, the policy will lapse unless the owner has signed up for an automatic premium loan or partial surrender of paid-up life insurance coverage. Under the automatic premium loan election, a policyowner authorizes an insurance company to use the policy's available cash value as collateral to secure a loan from the insurance company that is used to pay the scheduled premium. Loan interest is also charged to the cash value. When the cash value can no longer cover accumulated premium loans and interest, the policy lapses. The policyowner will then have no further coverage.

If partial surrender of paid-up insurance is elected, an insurance company will surrender enough units of paid-up insurance coverage at the end of the grace period to pay for the scheduled premium. The partial surrender decreases the net coverage amount. Since the guaranteed cash value of the base policy cannot be surrendered in part, the policy will lapse when all paid-up insurance has been depleted. At that time, the policyowner still has the base policy's guaranteed cash value which can be disposed of as cash, reduced paid-up insurance or extended term insurance.

Under the reduced paid-up insurance option, the guaranteed cash value is applied toward the purchase of single-premium permanent life insurance. The coverage is reduced, but will last for the remaining lifetime of the insured. Under the extended term insurance option, the guaranteed cash value is used to buy term insurance with the same coverage amount as the base policy. The duration of coverage is a function of the amount of guaranteed cash value, face amount, and age of the insured.

The previous examples are referred to as standard non-forfeiture options and are offered by almost every insurance company. Some insurance companies may offer additional options.

Paid-up Insurance Rider

To enhance policy performance, most insurance companies offer a paid-up insurance rider. It operates very much like a paid-up life insurance dividend option. The commission payable on the rider is much lower than that which is payable on the base policy itself. By combining sufficient units of paid-up insurance rider with the base policy, the policyowner can reduce the effective commission rate and thereby enhance returns on the insurance policy.

INTEREST-SENSITIVE WHOLE LIFE

Traditional whole life products are sometimes referred to as "bundled" products. Because insurance companies perform dividend calculations internally, and report the results to policyowners as single sums, there is no way owners can determine expense levels, investment returns, and the effective charges made for mortality. Since they have no information on rates of return, they can easily be tempted to surrender the policy during a period of rising interest rates, as happened during the late 1970s and early 1980s.

In an attempt to retain business during periods of rising interest rates, the insurance industry developed the interest-sensitive whole life policy, also known as excess interest whole life. With this policy, a buyer receives a guaranteed, or tabular, schedule of minimum cash values and death benefits which are based on a four percent interest rate and 1980 CSO Mortality Table, just like traditional whole life policies. The distinguishing trait of the interest-sensitive policy is the creation of a paper account called an accumulation account used to determine current, as opposed to guaranteed, cash values.

The accumulation account begins with a value of zero at issue. When the first premium is paid, front-end charges are deducted and the balance is credited to the account. At the beginning of each policy month, mortality charges and other charges specified in the contract, such as the policy administration fee, are deducted from the account. At the end of each policy month, interest is credited on the account balance. The interest rate is declared by an insurance company at the beginning of each policy year, and is usually applicable for the entire policy year even though the insurance company may change the rate credited to new policies. The account value is updated on a monthly basis.

At any given time, a policyowner's cash value is equal to the accumulation account balance less any back-end surrender charges. The surrender charge is typically based on a decreasing schedule so that after ten years it disappears. The surrender charge is designed to allow the insurance company to recoup a portion or all of the first year's unrecovered expenses. The current cash value is never less than the tabular cash value specified in the contract.

This type of product adds a variable interest component to the return provided by a permanent life insurance policy. In this regard, interest-sensitive whole life is markedly different from traditional whole life. However, just like traditional whole life, premiums must be paid when due to keep the policy in force, unless the policyowner has elected to use an automatic premium loan or a premium vanish.

Automatic Premium Loan and Premium Vanish

Non-forfeiture options are available with interest-sensitive whole life like those offered with traditional whole life insurance. The automatic premium loan feature is the same under both forms of insurance.

Under the premium vanish option, an insurance company projects the current cash value out to age 100, assuming no future premiums are paid. A comparison is made at each future policy anniversary between the projected current cash value and the tabular cash value. As long as the projected current cash value is equal to or greater than the tabular cash value at every future policy anniversary, a policyowner may suspend premium payment for the upcoming policy year. This process is repeated at every policy anniversary to determine whether the owner may continue to suspend premium payment. Insurance companies offer several variations of this option.

UNIVERSAL LIFE

Universal life was first introduced in 1979. It was developed to provide policyowners a flexible product that can easily be restructured to meet changing insurance needs. Universal life now accounts for a significant portion of in-force permanent life insurance.

Under a universal life policy, an insurance company maintains an accumulation account for determining cash value. Universal life has a flexible premium, meaning that a policyowner may pay premiums at will, within certain limits. Premiums are credited to the accumulation account after deducting for premium loads. Mortality charges and other expenses are deducted from the account at the beginning of each policy month, and interest is credited at the end of each policy month. The cash value is equal to the accumulation account balance less any applicable surrender charge.

Insurance companies do not guarantee a schedule of minimum cash values or death benefits under universal life. Instead, they guarantee that they will neither charge more than the 1980 CSO Mortality Table in mortality charges nor credit less than four percent interest in calculating the accumulation account balance. Further, expense loads charged to the account cannot exceed those allowed under state insurance regulations. Insurance companies must disclose interest rates and expenses.

A universal life insurance policy will stay in force as long as the accumulation account balance is sufficient at the beginning of each policy month to pay a mortality charge and other expenses. An insurance company sends a policyowner a notice of impending lapse if there is an insufficient balance in the account. At the end of each policy year, an insurer sends a statement disclosing charges and credits made to the accumulation account over the preceding twelve months.

An owner of a universal life policy need not follow any schedule of premium payment as long as there is sufficient value in the owner's account to pay the next month's mortality charge and other expenses. However, there are limits to premium flexibility.

An insurance company typically requires policyowners to make a minimum payment before it will issue the policy. Some insurance companies also require payment of small premiums for a specified period of time, such as three to five years, to keep a policy in force.

Moreover, policyowners cannot pay premiums exceeding those allowed under Section 7702 of the Internal Revenue Code (see Appendix F). If they exceed these limits, contracts will not qualify as life insurance and policyowners will lose all tax advantages associated with life insurance.

With universal life, the default non-forfeiture option is extended term insurance. A policyowner may trigger this option just by not paying premiums. Alternatively, the owner may elect a cash distribution or reduced paid-up insurance.

VARIABLE LIFE INSURANCE

Variable life insurance was introduced in the United States in 1976 after gaining acceptance in Europe. Variable life allows policyowners to invest in a variety of asset funds, potentially offsetting the adverse effects of inflation on life insurance policy values. Variable life investment options now include:

- Money market funds
- Bond funds
- High yield bond funds
- Common stock funds
- Growth stock funds
- Income funds
- Global equity funds
- Global bond funds
- Real estate funds
- Precious metal funds
- Asset allocation funds

Common stocks are viewed as an effective long-run hedge against inflation. However, the short-run returns of stock are volatile. Banks generally may not invest in stocks, putting the equity options in variable life off limits to them. For that reason, a variety of investments are available through variable life suitable for buyers with different regulatory circumstances and levels of risk tolerance.

In a variable life insurance policy, premiums minus expense loads and mortality charges are placed in one or more investment accounts, as directed by a policyowner, within certain limits. The death benefit and the cash value of a policy vary according to investment results or, put another way, the fair market value of the subaccounts. Typically, the death benefit does not fall below a guaranteed minimum. However, there is no minimum guarantee for the cash value. Therefore, variable life insurance passes all investment risk from an insurance company to a policyowner. The insurance company retains the expense and mortality risk.

In addition to the restrictions of state insurance laws and regulations, variable life insurance is subject to regulation by the Securities and Exchange Commission and must adhere to federal securities laws, including The Securities Act of 1933, The Securities Exchange Act of 1934, and The Investment Company Act of 1940.

The Securities Act of 1933 and Securities Exchange Act of 1934

The Securities Act of 1933 mandates registration requirements for new securities. These requirements are designed to provide investors with the information they need to make intelligent decisions about securities purchases. Variable life investments are treated as securities under law. As issuer of the security, an insurance company must file a registration statement with the SEC and prepare a prospectus for distribution to prospective investors. This prospectus must disclose the nature of the insurance company, fees and expenses to be charged under the variable life insurance policy, and the policyowner's rights.

The Securities Exchange Act of 1934 regulates the secondary securities market. Under this law, a firm that distributes variable life insurance must register as a broker-dealer. All broker-dealers and persons associated with the sale of variable life insurance must register with the National Association of Securities Dealers and pass a securities examination. In addition, the 1934 Act requires periodic disclosure by insurance companies to policyowners.

The Investment Company Act of 1940

Under the Investment Company Act of 1940, a variable life insurance separate account, composed of various investment subaccounts, and corresponding investment funds, must register as investment companies. Typically, the separate account is registered as open-end diversified management investment companies. The 1940 act also regulates the management and operation of these investment companies, sets maximum sales charges, and requires the investment companies to distribute periodic financial reports.

Private Placement Variable Life Insurance

In recent years, many insurance companies have begun to offer a new type of variable life insurance known as private placement variable life insurance. Private placement variable life insurance is exempt from registration requirements under Rule 506, part of Regulation D of the Securities Act of 1933. Under the act, an insurance company must ensure that a prospective policyowner is an accredited investor or an unaccredited investor who "...has such knowledge and experience in financial and business matters that he is capable of evaluating the merits and risks of the prospective investment."

Accredited investors include institutional investors, such as banks and mutual funds, and wealthy individuals. An insurance company can sell to no more than 35 unaccredited purchasers who meet the rule's criteria. In addition, Rule 506 prohibits insurance companies from publicly marketing private placement products.

Private placement variable life insurance is designed mainly for large institutional buyers. Loads, charges, and policy provisions are negotiated between buyers and insurance companies within the constraints of state insurance regulations.

An insurance company usually will allow buyers to select one or more outside investment managers in place of the company or any of its subsidiaries to manage all or part of a policy's assets. Insurance companies normally will sell private placement variable life insurance and permit outside investment managers only for large accounts above a minimum case size; that is, $1,000,000 of premium.

INSURANCE COMPANY INVESTMENT STRATEGIES

In order to be able to honor their obligations to policyowners, insurance companies structure their investment portfolios to produce cash flows that closely mirror their liabilities. The structure of their liabilities reflects the types of insurance products they sell.

General Account Life Insurance

General account life insurance products promise fixed-dollar benefits. The best types of assets to match this liability are fixed income securities. Since fixed-dollar benefit liabilities are backed by the general account, the insurance company invests a major portion of its general account assets in investment-grade bonds and mortgages.

For example, one life insurance company maintains a portfolio in its general account distributed as shown below:

Government Bonds	18.2%
Other Bonds	47.2%
Mortgages	20.0%
Stocks and Real Estate	1.2%
Cash and Cash Equivalents	1.1%
Policy Loans	12.3%

The bond quality of the company is weighted heavily toward the investment-grade end of the quality spectrum as illustrated by the following table:

AAA	36.8%
AA	12.2%
A	30.8%
BBB	17.8%
BB or lower	2.4%

This type of general account asset mix is fairly typical of financially strong life insurance companies.

Separate Account Life Insurance

An insurance company typically maintains one separate account to hold the assets that support the liabilities generated by its separate account life insurance policies. This holding is in addition to any other separate accounts it may maintain to support other variable-dollar benefit liabilities.

An owner of a separate account life insurance policy can select investment subaccounts into which net premiums are to be deposited. The death benefit and cash value of a separate account life insurance policy reflect the fair market value of the underlying investment subaccounts chosen by the policyowner.

A policyowner of a separate account life insurance contract can choose any combination of investment subaccounts offered by the contract. In turn, an insurance company invests the assets of each subaccount in a corresponding investment fund. The investment funds are series type mutual funds registered with the Securities and Exchange Commission as open-end diversified management investment companies under the Investment Company Act of 1940. The policyowner, rather than the insurance company, determines the portfolio mix. Managers of the series funds control trading of securities, operating within the constraints of the investment objectives and policies set for the particular funds that they manage.

PRODUCT PRICING

The ultimate goal of product pricing is to ensure that the present value of future premiums is at least equal to the sum of the present values of benefit costs, policy expenses, allocated fixed expenses, and required profits.

When an insurance company develops a new product, the company's actuaries run the proposed product through a pricing model. Every insurance company has instituted its own profitability targets as measured by:

- Return on investment
- Premium margin
- Break-even year
- First year surplus strain

To the extent that the initial product design does not meet profitability objectives, actuaries and marketing specialists work jointly to modify the product design to optimize the trade-off between product appeal and profitability. The variables subject to change during this process are pricing assumptions and schedules for death benefits and cash values.

The expected timing of profits and losses must also be considered. The key variables to be considered on a block of new business include:

- Age and sex distribution
- Face amount distribution
- Risk distribution
- Policy lapses
- Mortality
- Investment returns
- Variable expenses
- Fixed expenses

Other factors that affect product pricing include an insurance company's reserving philosophy, sales goals, surplus position, and access to capital.

Deterministic and Stochastic Techniques of Pricing

Insurance companies use a variety of techniques in pricing products. These techniques can be categorized as either deterministic or stochastic. Many techniques combine elements of both methods.

A deterministic approach focuses on the most likely combination of future events based on past experience. The actuary bases his or her assumptions about what outcomes are likely in the future on an insurance company's experience with similar groups.

By contrast, a stochastic approach is based entirely on probability. An actuary makes assumptions about the statistical distribution underlying each variable. A random event generator is then developed to create a large number of possible scenarios based on assumed underlying distributions. Product profitability is calculated for each scenario. After perhaps 10,000 runs have been simulated, results can be plotted from which the actuary can develop fairly accurate projections of the profitability of the product. For example, the actuary may conclude there is a 90 percent probability that the ultimate profit for a proposed product will not be less than x million dollars and the first year loss will not exceed y million.

Of those techniques that combine the two approaches, the most common is a method in which an insurance company determines a set number of scenarios it considers to be most likely, assigning a probability to each. Profitability for each scenario is calculated. Based on the assigned probabilities, the insurance company calculates a probability-weighted profitability for the product. If the weighted profitability calculation meets all of the insurance company's targets, the product will be introduced.

PRODUCT CAPACITY

In the traditional marketplace, insurance companies try to maximize product sales. However, this effort is not the case in the BOLI market for two reasons: surplus strain and disintermediation risk.

Insurance companies typically suffer a first-year loss from the issuance of a new policy. The loss is the result of many one-time expenses associated with the sale of a policy, such as selling, underwriting, issuance, and record setup. An insurance company must have enough unallocated surplus to absorb these first-year losses. If not, it must limit its sales or accept deterioration in its surplus position.

Under normal circumstances, no single buyer can purchase enough coverage to exhaust an insurance company's surplus set aside for new sales in a given year. However, in the BOLI market, an insurance company can easily exhaust an entire year's allocation of surplus in a few large transactions, preventing it from accepting any new business. Thus, an insurance company must divide its available surplus between its regular business and BOLI, effectively limiting the number of BOLI transactions in any one year.

Equally important in determining how much BOLI an insurance company may sell is potential disintermediation risk. Such risk is not an issue with variable life insurance because the value of the liability is equal to the value of the assets. Therefore, an insurance company is not at risk should it be forced to liquidate the assets to pay off its liabilities.

However, general account life insurance, which promises fixed-dollar benefits, does present disintermediation risk. Since an insurance company invests primarily in fixed-income securities, it faces disintermediation risk in a rising interest rate environment. Although asset values fluctuate, liabilities associated with portfolio insurance are measured at book value, which never decreases, regardless of interest rates.

Thus, if a bank were to decide to cash in its BOLI program to take advantage of rising market interest rates, the insurance company would have to liquidate fixed-income securities in a rising interest rate environment, likely generating a capital loss. The gap between the book value of liabilities and the market value of assets would have to be made up from the insurance company's surplus, impairing the company's surplus position.

An insurance company can shorten the duration of its fixed income portfolio to reduce interest rate sensitivity. However, by going shorter on the yield curve, returns to BOLI buyers are reduced, diminishing the product's appeal. Therefore, insurance companies in the BOLI market have placed limits on the amount of new business they will accept in any given year.

CHAPTER 4
FINANCIAL PERFORMANCE OF BOLI

This chapter discusses the historical and prospective yields of BOLI compared with traditional bank investments. BOLI is evaluated on both an after-tax and pre-tax basis. Since BOLI yields are income tax-free if policies are held to maturity, investment returns should be measured on a tax-free basis.

It is easy to construct a historical performance of BOLI. Life insurance carriers maintain careful performance records. For many life insurance carriers, their historical yield is a strong selling point. Carrier yields can be matched against yields from traditional bank investments to arrive at comparisons.

The chart on page 65 compares, over a multiple year period, a type of traditional portfolio life insurance available through BOLI and a selection of traditional bank investments. BOLI has a yield advantage in every year.

BOLI's yield advantage is easy to understand. The insurance carrier is investing in a seven- to 10-year duration investment. The carrier passes on that yield—minus their charges—income tax-free.

While the data show that BOLI offers higher yields than traditional bank investments, other considerations must be taken into account before setting up a BOLI plan. BOLI is different in some important respects from traditional bank investments in areas such as duration, liquidity and taxation.

ANNUAL PORTFOLIO YIELD BOLI VS AFTER-TAX INVESTMENT YIELDS

Historical Alternative Investment vs. Actual BOLI Yield

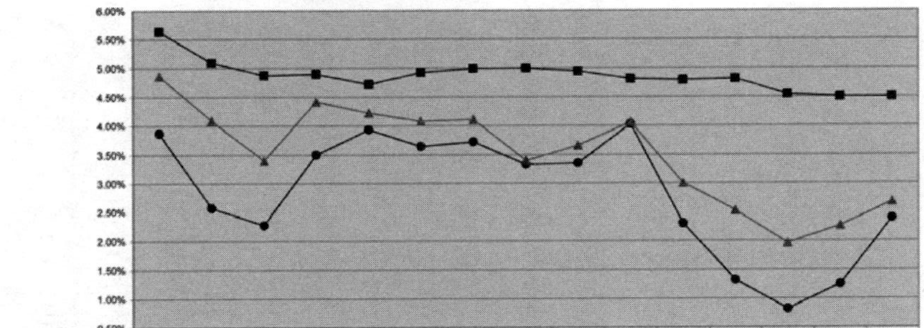

	1991	1992	1993	1994	1995	1996	1997	1998	1999	2000	2001	2002	2003	2004	2005
1-Yr Treasuries	3.87%	2.57%	2.27%	3.50%	3.93%	3.64%	3.72%	3.33%	3.35%	4.03%	2.30%	1.32%	0.82%	1.25%	2.39%
5-Yr Treasuries	4.86%	4.08%	3.40%	4.41%	4.22%	4.08%	4.11%	3.40%	3.66%	4.06%	3.00%	2.52%	1.96%	2.26%	2.67%
BOLI Yield	5.63%	5.10%	4.87%	4.90%	4.72%	4.92%	4.99%	5.00%	4.94%	4.81%	4.79%	4.81%	4.54%	4.50%	4.50%

This simplified comparison is intended to show actual historical yields on BOLI versus other investments a bank typically makes. It is not meant to be a full comparison of all differences between BOLI and such other investments, such as differences in liquidity, safety or fluctuation of principal. For example, Federal Funds and Treasuries are guaranteed by the U.S. Government. In addition, Federal Funds and Treasuries are of shorter duration than BOLI; therefore yields tend to be lower.

(1) Treasury rates are from Federal Reserve Statistical Release H.15 dated 1/10/06, net of Federal taxes at an assumed rate of 34.00%, exclusive of any transactions costs.
(2) BOLI Yield reflects the current tax-preferred treatment on cash value life insurance. BOLI Yield is based on actual Clark Consulting experience for general account products for a 45-year-old, nonsmoking male, and is the effective annual yield for the yield measurement period. The yield for each year is the average of the actual yields, net of loads and mortality expenses, of representative policies issued in that year, which remained in-force (i.e. no surrenders or death claims) throughout the yield measurement period. For years 1991 through 2000, the measurement period is the first five full policy years. For years 2001 through 2005, the measurement period is from policy issue to their most recent policy anniversary that actual values are available. General account products have a guaranteed minimum return. Separate account products generally have no guaranteed crediting rate and may be subject to market fluctuations; see the Prospectus or Private Placement Memorandum for further details.

Securities products and services are offered through Clark Securities Inc.,
DBA CCFS, Inc. in Texas, 633 West Fifth Street, 52nd Floor, Los Angeles, CA 90071-2086.
Ph: 213-438-6300. Member NASD & SIPC

DURATION

BOLI is a long-term investment strategy. It is used to finance benefit costs which, by their nature, are long term. In fact, benefit plan costs can effectively be considered permanent costs. As long as a bank is in business, it will have significant benefit costs. Therefore, the long-term nature of BOLI is appropriate. In effect, BOLI can be viewed as a perpetual municipal with a yield that resets to the market annually. And, as yield comparisons demonstrate, the after-tax performance advantage of BOLI is favorable both in the short- and long-term.

LIQUIDITY

BOLI is a liquid investment. However, the best investment strategy is to hold BOLI to maturity when death proceeds are paid income tax-free. That makes the tax benefits permanent. Should coverage be terminated before the death of the insured, the cash value paid at surrender in excess of the premium is taxable as ordinary income to the bank. Therefore, it is to a bank's advantage to hold contracts to maturity. All the same, a tax-deferred yield is normally preferable to a yield that is taxable annually, just like tax-deferred annuities have advantages over certificates of deposit on any typical investment that is taxed annually.

Since the investment yield of BOLI is attractive in comparison to alternative bank investment opportunities, the liquidity issue should not normally arise. Banks would not ordinarily need to tap BOLI's cash value. Banks generally will not put more than three percent of their assets in BOLI. Therefore, BOLI should be considered a last-resort store of liquidity. Any bank that would have to turn to BOLI for liquidity would probably be experiencing earnings problems and not owe income taxes. Although surrender of BOLI would create a taxable event, that event would be immaterial since the bank would probably not be in a taxpaying status.

The issue of liquidity varies depending on the type of insurance policy the bank buys. Under the Internal Revenue Code, there are two methods of taxation applicable to life insurance contracts: the Non-Modified Endowment Contract and the Modified Endowment Contract.

TAXATION: NON-MODIFIED ENDOWMENT CONTRACT

Under a Non-Modified Endowment Contract, a bank must pay at least four level premiums. The face amount of the insurance will be approximately 25 times the annual premium.

Under the contract, a bank can borrow on a nontaxable basis, according to the policy's cash value. For example, if the cash value were $10 million, a bank would be able to borrow that amount from the carrier. The interest rate charged on loans is set annually and tied to the Moody's bond rate for seasoned corporate bonds.

Such loans are nonrecourse and have no scheduled payback date. Loans can remain outstanding indefinitely, repaid when insured people die, or when a policy is surrendered. Loans are not recorded as liabilities, but are netted against cash surrender values of contracts, which are bank assets. Therefore, loans do not affect bank debt/equity ratios.

Loans are made by carriers against cash surrender values of the contracts and are nontaxable to the bank. Any interest earnings on premiums paid are also tax-free. If a bank were to pay $10 million in premiums over four years, and the cash value of a contract at the end of the fourth year were $13 million, the entire amount, including principal and interest, could be borrowed on an income tax-free basis.

TAXATION: MODIFIED ENDOWMENT CONTRACT

Under a Modified Endowment Contract, a bank can pay as little as one premium. With a single premium contract, a bank will have a smaller death benefit in comparison to its premium. The average face amount may be only four to five times the premium. This reduced face amount helps a bank since it would pay a smaller mortality charge. Since a modified endowment contract can still qualify as life insurance under the code and have a face amount which is less than that required with a Non-Modified Endowment Contract, the early year performance of the contract is superior, providing a higher first year cash value and, thus, yield.

However, the taxation of a Modified Endowment Contract is different. Loans taken against policy cash value are treated as interest income and taxable. A 10-percent tax applies on loan interest earnings and upon surrender.

A reasonable question to ask is, should a bank simply buy Non-Modified Endowment Contracts in order to have access to policy cash value in a tax favored manner? The non-modified endowment contract has a higher face amount requirement and the corresponding mortality charges for additional death benefit. Moreover, the internal rate of returns in the earlier years is lower.

For banks concerned about early yield, the modified endowment contract clearly offers superior performance in the early years. If a bank does not expect to use BOLI contracts for liquidity, it is more advantageous to use a Modified Endowment Contract.

CHAPTER 5
SEPARATE ACCOUNT LIFE INSURANCE

Bank-Owned Life Insurance (BOLI) has its roots back in the early 1980s. Community banks began purchasing single premium and annual premium universal life insurance policies to fund benefits for their officers. These policies were uniquely designed insurance products that credited a fixed rate of interest to the cash value.

EVOLUTION OF LIFE INSURANCE IN BOLI MARKET

The product was designed such that the initial cash value was equal to the premium paid and then grew with interest. The interest rate was guaranteed never to be less than a specified annual rate generally in the 4.00 percent range. The policy was designed always to be accretive to the policyholder. With an increasing cash value the policyholder only has a positive P&L impact. Of course, a charge for the mortality risk being assumed by the insurance carrier was also charged against the cash value. These general account policies were generally written in increments of $1 million or less. In the late 1980s and early 1990s, larger banks discovered the advantages of BOLI, and began purchasing larger amounts of general account policies.

General account policies refer to the fact that the investments supporting the cash value of the policies reside in an insurance company's general account. Assets in the general account are invested according to each carrier's investment guidelines, and may include corporate bonds, private placement bonds, equities, ABS, and MBS securities.

Based on the investment performance and the carrier's expense structure, the carrier declares an interest rate to be credited to the cash value of the policies subject to the minimum rate guarantees. Because the actual investment return and expenses are unknown to the client, some people have called these general account products a black box. On the positive side, the general account products guarantee that the policyowner will receive their full cash value upon surrender regardless of any asset defaults, capital losses or the actual market value of assets in the general account. In addition, the diversified nature of the general account assets may provide attractive returns. However, the policyholder is only a general creditor of the carrier in the event the carrier gets into financial difficulties.

The mid to late 1990s saw the arrival of separate account life insurance policies into the marketplace. The evolution of stable value wraps from the GIC market made the sale of separate account life insurance products viable to the banking world.

By nature, separate account product has a variable return. The total return of the underlying assets is passed through to the policyholder. That return may be positive or negative. The cash value may increase or decrease causing uncertain P&L treatment for a bank. The stable value wrap smoothes out the volatility, and is designed to create an accretive policy similar to the general account design. The stable value wrap feature and others made separate account a viable alternative to general account products. While each product has its merits and detractions, the proper choice is up to each bank and its specific requirements. The remainder of this chapter discusses separate account policies in more detail.

SEPARATE ACCOUNT LIFE INSURANCE

Separate account life insurance is an unbundled form of permanent life insurance. Like all permanent (as opposed to term) insurance, a premium is paid to the insurance carrier, a cash value is created and a death benefit is paid upon death. Under most circumstances, if the policy is properly structured from a regulatory standpoint, the earnings on the cash value are tax-deferred until withdrawal and the death benefits (including the cash value earnings) are tax-free.

A number of items make separate account life insurance different from general account (commonly called universal life or whole life) life insurance. The main difference involves the cash values of the policies.

As discussed previously, the cash values of a general account policy are supported by the general investments of the insurance carrier. A separate account policy offers multiple investment options within a "separate account" to the policyholder to support the cash value of the policy. The policyholder may choose to have the cash value invested in bond funds, equity funds or many other types of funds. Of course, a bank must consider bank eligibility guidelines. The policyholder's cash value then increases or decreases based on the performance of the underlying investment options chosen. A discussion of stable value wrappers that create a more stable return is included later in this chapter.

Another feature of separate account life insurance is that the separate account created by the insurance company for this purpose is isolated from the general creditors of the insurance company. Only liabilities associated with the separate account can be charged to the separate account. This feature helps reduce the credit risk that a policyholder may have to the insurance company. On the flip side, this feature exposes the policyholder directly to the performance of the investment option chosen, including capital gains and losses, unrealized gains and losses, and asset defaults. There are no minimum interest guarantees as in most general account (universal life) insurance policies. Purchasing separate account life insurance has been compared to being invested in mutual funds.

Separate account life insurance is highly regulated both as insurance and as a security. The main concerns are ensuring that the policy qualifies as life insurance under state law. Only life insurance that meets the test of IRC Code Section 7702 and 7702A receive the tax advantages afforded life insurance. Also IRC Code Section 817 contains rules regarding diversification of investments within the insurance, as well as investor-control issues that must be followed to qualify the policies as life insurance and receive the appropriate tax treatment under IRC Section 101. This book does not provide tax, legal or accounting advice on any of these topics.

MAJOR COMPONENTS OF SEPARATE ACCOUNT LIFE INSURANCE USED FOR BOLI

Three main components generally constitute a separate account BOLI product. The base insurance policy provides the chassis for this insurance vehicle. The fund options available provide the fuel that drives the insurance vehicle. An optional stable value wrapper acts as a governor moderating and controlling the variability of the product performance.

The insurance chassis provides the framework for the entire product. The chassis dictates the product pricing, the regulatory requirements and, importantly, the mortality mechanism for paying death benefits—the real reason for the policy in the first place.

A number of carriers provide product chassis to the BOLI marketplace. Because of the limited risks to the carrier to underwrite separate account BOLI policies (no minimum interest rate guarantees, no asset default guarantees, no full book value guarantees), the carriers essentially have an unlimited capacity for premium.

The pricing for the separate account life insurance chassis is very institutionalized and, hence, competitive. Typically, the carriers will charge a very modest asset-based fee to recover their expenses and profits. This fee is usually referred to as the Mortality and Expense Charge (M&E). While the term includes "mortality," this fee does not actually cover the true probability and costs of paying out the death benefits. The true charge for the actual mortality risk is recovered in the "Cost of Insurance" (COI). The COI is generally a monthly charge based on the demographics of the group and charged relative to the amount of death benefits, not assets.

Expenses also covered in the product chassis will include a charge to recover premium taxes (a state tax) and Deferred Acquisition Cost (DAC) taxes (a federal tax). These costs may be charged in explicit or implicit ways through the product, the stable value wrapper, or even in some creative reserving methods. No matter what the methodology, there is a true cost involved and the purchaser must be very diligent in understanding where this cost is charged in their policy.

A carrier may also charge administration fees or other "risk" charges. In addition, a fee is also charged to pay a broker to market, sell, implement and service the BOLI program. There are additional fees for investment management and stable value wrap protection that are discussed separately in this chapter.

The bottom line: A purchaser must consider the policy pricing in its totality. Carriers may take different charges in different areas to cover their expenses. Purchasers would be doing a great disservice to themselves by only focusing on one element of the pricing such as an M&E charge. We have seen policy chassis with high M&E's outperform chassis with much lower M&E fees, due to other elements of the pricing.

Additionally, some carriers express their fees in different manners, such as annual equivalents, bond equivalents or monthly fees. Again, the purchaser must be very careful to avoid the pitfalls of merely looking at expenses, in the belief that he or she is comparing apples to apples. Full disclosure of all product costs, and exactly how they will be charged, is critical.

MORTALITY

Even though life insurance is being purchased, the actual mechanics of the death benefits are one of the least understood elements of an insurance policy, but one of the most important. The cornerstone of life insurance is that risk (mortality) must be transferred to another party and redistributed among other policyholders.

In practice, the insurance company charges a cost of insurance, similar to a term insurance premium, based on the amount of insurance, age, sex, and possibly smoking status of each insured. The cost of insurance is generally based on the probability of that insured person dying in the given period. If the insured dies, a death benefit is paid that is in excess of the cost of insurance. If the insured survives the period, the insurance company keeps the cost of insurance. The insurance company may use the cost of insurance to pay death benefits to a completely different policyholder. This element is the risk shifting and risk distribution.

Many types of mortality mechanisms exist in the BOLI market. The most basic is standard or sometimes called pooled mortality. The pooled structure works as explained in the previous paragraph. Some banks are concerned that death benefits create lumpiness in their earnings streams. A large death benefit can create a significant amount of income in a given period. Additionally, some banks are concerned that the insurance company may overcharge for mortality. As a result, some insurance companies introduced "experience-rating" mechanisms.

Experience rating was designed to level the earnings impact of death benefits, and also limit the insurance carriers' ability to overcharge for the cost of insurance. In the extreme sense, a policyholder would essentially pay only for their own claims. The risk-shifting and risk-distribution principle could be called into question under an extreme experience rated example. Other variations exist that require implementing stop loss coverage and other techniques.

Policyholders must be satisfied that the policy they are purchasing will qualify as life insurance; that is, there is bonafide risk transfer and risk distribution. Without those elements, if the policy is disqualified as insurance, all the tax benefits will vanish. Additionally, accounting issues must be considered depending on the treatment of claims reserves that may be included in an experience-rated program. Finally, there may be hidden costs in experience rating ranging from "retention" charges (an added carrier fee) to lost interest on a claims reserve, which could amount to numerous annual basis points of cost.

SEPARATE ACCOUNT FUND OPTIONS

Within the separate account chassis, the policyholder is able to select how the cash value will be invested. As mentioned previously, the investment fund provides the fuel, the earnings, for the insurance chassis. Generally, the policyholder may select from a number of "mutual fund like" options. These options may range from money market funds to MBS strategies, bond strategies, portable alpha strategies, and hedge fund strategies. The cash value of the insurance policy is invested in the selected fund. The cash value then is credited earnings (or losses) based on the actual performance of the fund option. Policy expenses from the chassis are then deducted from the overall cash value to determine the periodic return.

A separate chapter explores the various fund options generally available. The fund selection is the most critical element of the policy selection. Whereas chassis expenses may only vary by a few basis points from company to company, the investment return from different investment managers and strategies may create significant return differences.

Separate account life insurance must also abide by certain restrictions and regulation on the investment front to preserve life insurance tax treatment. Specifically, each investment option must meet IRC Section 817(h) diversification requirements. These requirements are outlined in the Appendix. Secondly, the insurance company must legally own all the assets. The policyholder cannot be perceived to be the owner of the assets. This principle is covered under IRC Section 817(d) and numerous pronouncements by the IRS. The "investor-control" doctrine is still somewhat a subjective area, but purchasers must be aware of and abide by the guidelines to avoid tax challenges in the future.

The purchaser should consider whether the investment options are bank eligible, with the appropriate risk weighting and management style, as he or she would in any investment under purchase consideration. Because the investment returns are passed through to the policyholder, the regulatory authorities have determined that a policyholder should "look-through" to the underlying assets to determine bank eligibility and risk weights. The Interagency Statement outlines appropriate methods for determining the appropriate risk weighting. Finally, a purchaser must consider the fund expenses, risk/return profile, and appropriateness of the strategy relative to the bank's other investments.

STABLE VALUE WRAP

The stable value wrap acts as a governor or regulator on the returns from the investment options chosen. A separate account product passes on the direct return of the investment options chosen. This direct return includes gains and losses and the volatility associated with a total return. A fund may return 10 percent one year, and negative 5 percent the next. This market volatility can cause problems for the bank. A bank prefers a constantly accretive asset similar to general account products. To solve this problem, stable value wrappers migrated from the pension market to the BOLI market.

A stable value wrap is designed to pass through the actual total return of the fund option it wraps, over the lifetime of the product, less the expense of the wrapper. However, the "stable" portion is designed to smooth out the periodic volatility of good years and bad years. For instance, if the fund described above had a stable value wrapper, the bank would receive a 7.5 percent return for two years, instead of the volatile actual return. This example is highly simplified to make the point.

The other main purpose of a stable value wrap is to provide book value accounting. If the market value of the fund option decreases below the carrying value (cash value or book value), the wrap provider guarantees to pay the difference between actual market value and the appropriate book value upon a policy surrender. According to FASB TB 85-4, the amount available on surrender at the valuation date is the amount to be carried on the bank's books. The stable value wrapper creates the funds to provide the bank with stable, book value accounting within limits. Additionally, the wrapper generally guarantees that interest of at least equal to zero percent, before expenses, will be credited to the cash value each period.

Actually, the stable value wrap becomes an asset in each fund option wrapped, and is a contract between the insurance company and the wrap provider. The policyholder is not a party to this transaction as that could create investor-control issues.

Finally, the wrapper contract dictates how interest will be credited to the policy cash value. The formula translates the actual total return of the fund over time into a stable credited rate to the cash value. A bank should clearly understand how each wrap formula works. These formulas have the flexibility to create temporary artificial rate enhancements, cash value enhancements and mechanisms to amortize taxes and other expenses. Actually, some formulas can create unstable rates because certain formula features that create artificial crediting-rate formulas may disintegrate under certain circumstances.

The potential purchaser should also understand the limits of the wrapper. The wrapper provides a guarantee to make up the difference between market value and book value, but only up to a specific differential. The differential ranges from 10 percent to 20 percent, depending on the underlying fund option. If greater volatility occurs, the wrapper could become ineffective or create book value write-downs or force asset reallocations.

The pricing for stable value wrappers varies by provider, the fund option strategy and volatility and internal provisions of the wrapper. The purchaser needs to understand the various legal provisions of the wrapper that dictate liquidity of the fund (when can the policy be surrendered or exchanged or funds transferred to other funds). Certain requirements exist for surrender and 1035 exchanges that require the scrutiny of the potential purchaser.

ADVANTAGES AND DISADVANTAGES OF SEPARATE ACCOUNT

Separate account is a natural evolution to general account in the BOLI market. General account provided stable returns with very strong guarantees and minimal risks to the purchaser. These general account policies still provide great value to the bank that wants strong guarantees and certainty in their BOLI program. With a greater emphasis on the investment world, and some concerns about a bank's exposure to credit risk with an insurance company, separate account life insurance is a natural extension.

Separate account provides explicit expenses, potentially lower expenses than general account, explicit top-line returns due to the transparent fund options, and less credit risk to the carrier. However, all good things come with a negative side. Separate account does not provide minimum interest rate guarantees (the stable value wrap provides a 0 percent guarantee), only protects the difference between book and market up to a certain amount, whereas general account provides 100 percent protection and directly passes through investment risks, such as asset defaults. The prospective purchaser should evaluate all the risk/return elements when making a final decision between types of insurance, as well as the providers of the insurance.

CHAPTER 6
How To Select A BOLI Carrier

Once a bank has decided to set up a BOLI plan, it is vital to find competitive and creditworthy insurance carrier or carriers. BOLI policies are not off-the-shelf products. Custom-tailored plan design and pricing are needed to achieve optimum results.

To serve the BOLI market, an insurance company must have a significant surplus. Among those carriers in a position to sell BOLI, only a few have made a commitment to the market or set up special departments to sell life insurance to banks. The relatively small number of providers makes selection simpler.

In choosing an insurance company, there are several factors that should be considered:

- Financial strength
- Plan type
- Pricing and projected returns
- Limits on policy amounts
- Account management
- Ability to administer BOLI

FINANCIAL STRENGTH

The most effective way to measure an insurance carrier is through rating systems designed by industry watchdogs, such as A.M. Best Company, Standard & Poor's and Moody's. Each firm has its own method of rating insurance companies. The following chart shows the rating systems used by each of the three:

INSURANCE CARRIER RATING AGENCIES AND RANKINGS

Ranking Level	A.M. Best*	Standard & Poor's**	Moody's ***
1	A++	AAA	Aaa
2	A+	AA+	Aa1
3	A	AA	Aa2
4	A-	AA-	Aa3
5	B++	A+	A1
6	B+	A	A2
7	B	A-	A3
8	B-	BBB+	Baa1
9	C++	BBB	Baa2
10	C+	BBB-	Baa3
11	C	BB+	Ba1
12	C-	BB	Ba2
13	D	BB-	Ba3
14	E	B+	B1
15	F	B	B2
16		B-	B3
17		CCC	Caa
18		R	Ca
19			C

*Rating based on "Insurance Claims Paying Ability."
**Rating based on "Company's Financial Strength and Ability to Meet Obligations to Policyholders."
***Rating based on "Degree of Investment Risk…Protected by a Stable Margin and Secure Principal."

> Carriers rated in the top four levels have minimal credit risk and are the best candidates to select when making a BOLI purchase.

PLAN TYPE

Insurance companies may design BOLI products in-house or use consultants with specialized expertise. Products that are backed by a carrier's general portfolio are usually designed by the company's own actuaries. Separate Account products may be designed in-house or by outside consultants. Hybrid forms of BOLI are unusual and are normally designed by outside firms.

> It may be in the bank's interest to hire a broker or consultant to assist in the design of hybrid plans. A good BOLI consultant employs actuaries and other professionals who have the specialized knowledge and skill, which hybrid products require. Consultants with proprietary products have particular leverage in dealing with insurance carriers.

PRICING

Pricing is a critical part of the design of a life insurance product. Setting prices is done in conjunction with the investment design portion of the plan. Figured into the price of a life insurance policy are mortality costs, cost of insurance, DAC taxes, fees, and commissions.

Carriers with large BOLI pools have the experience to price their products accurately. A newcomer to the market may be able to use its experience with other types of corporate life insurance to set prices.

When a carrier prices accurately, a bank's costs and benefits are optimized. If an insurance company underprices its products, a bank will not necessarily gain. The carrier may have to make up for the deficit in future years by increasing the cost of insurance. Funds used to make up for these shortcomings will reduce the amount of capital available for investment.

ACCOUNT MANAGEMENT

One of the most important factors in determining which carrier to select is the number and quality of investment accounts offered. There is considerable variation in the level of involvement of carriers in investment management. A bank can recommend an outside investment manager to the carrier. However, the bank may not exercise control over the investment manager's decisions. If a bank is dissatisfied with investment results, it may have the option of surrendering its policies. But the disadvantages of surrender—especially the loss of tax benefits—makes such a move undesirable. Conflict can be avoided by discussing investment management with a carrier before a purchase is made.

PLAN ADMINISTRATION

The administrative duties of a carrier include processing death claims and program accounting. The latter is especially important because a bank needs accurate information about its account balance in order to report its earnings. Choosing a carrier with the ability to properly administer a plan is essential.

CHAPTER 7
BOLI ACCOUNTING

Accounting is the process of identifying, measuring, recording, and communicating economic information to permit informed decisions by users of that information. When a bank makes a decision to purchase life insurance, it must comply with various regulatory accounting requirements. While most corporations are governed by Generally Accepted Accounting Principles (GAAP), banks are subject to additional accounting rules promulgated by state and federal bank regulatory agencies.

GENERALLY ACCEPTED ACCOUNTING PRINCIPLES (GAAP)

The American Institute of Certified Public Accountants (AICPA), the Financial Accounting Standards Board (FASB), and the Securities and Exchange Commission (SEC) are the agencies primarily responsible for developing GAAP. These accounting standards were developed to reduce inconsistencies in accounting practice and to improve the comparability and credibility of financial reports. Banks, like any other corporation, are required to prepare their financial statements in conformity with GAAP.

SECURITIES AND EXCHANGE COMMISSION

The SEC is an independent regulatory agency of the U.S. government, which administers the Securities Act of 1933, the Securities Exchange Act of 1934, and other legislation. It is empowered to require corporate reports including the following:

- Registration statements required when companies make public offerings of securities
- 10-K Reports, filed annually, which include audited financial statements
- 10-Q Reports, filed quarterly, which include financial information for the period
- 8-K Reports, which explain events about which investors should be aware

The SEC requires all registrants to conform with GAAP. Regulations S-X contain the SEC's principle accounting guidelines. Article 4, Reg. 210.4-01 (a) (1) states that:

> Financial statements filed with the Commission, which are not prepared in accordance with generally accepted accounting principles, will be presumed to be misleading or inaccurate…

According to GAAP, in reporting purchases of life insurance, changes in cash surrender value must be classified as adjustments to premium expense.

BANK REGULATORY AGENCIES

Banks are regulated by several federal and state agencies including the Office of the Comptroller of the Currency (OCC), the Federal Reserve System (Fed), the Federal Deposit Insurance Corporation (FDIC), and state banking departments. The Office of Thrift Supervision (OTS) has jurisdiction over savings institutions. These agencies issue charters and supervise commercial banks and thrifts.

Bank regulators have developed their own accounting regulations, referred to as Regulatory Accounting Principles (RAP), which can differ from GAAP. Bank regulators are concerned with safeguarding the safety and soundness of financial institutions and require certain financial information beyond that required by GAAP.

In some instances, RAP accounting methods are contrary to GAAP. In other instances, GAAP allows flexibility in accounting treatment, but RAP requires a specific method. Accounting for BOLI uses GAAP methods. There are no RAP guidelines that require treatment of BOLI different from that provided for by GAAP. However, state and federal bank regulatory agencies stress the need to monitor an insurance carrier's financial condition on an ongoing basis.

ACCOUNTING FOR BOLI

Accounting for bank purchase of life insurance is relatively simple.[1] A bank identifies certain key executives or employees on whom it wishes to purchase life insurance. The bank is both the owner and beneficiary of the insurance policies. An insurance carrier is selected to provide the coverage in an amount determined to be in line with the risk

[1]Although not addressed in this chapter, risk-based capital guidelines are discussed in Appendix C.

of loss or the present value of future employee benefit cost. The bank can pay a single premium or annual premiums.

Periodically, the insurance carrier reports to the bank the cash surrender value of the policies. The cash surrender value represents the gross cash value of the policy, adjusted for expenses, accumulated dividends, interest, and prepaid premiums. The increase in cash surrender values is considered income for financial accounting purposes, but may be netted against premium expenses.

In the event of the death of an insured, the insurance carrier pays the bank the death proceeds. This payment is recorded as income. Because the death causes a corresponding decrease in the cash surrender value, the bank must reverse out the cash surrender value related to the policy that has matured.

FASB TECHNICAL BULLETIN NO.85-4

(See Appendix B)

FASB Technical Bulletin No. 85-4, titled *Accounting for Purchases of Life Insurance,* is the primary accounting guide. It is effective for insurance policies acquired after November 14, 1985. This bulletin evolved from a 1970 AICPA accounting interpretation entitled *Accounting for Key-Man Life Insurance,* which identified the cash surrender value method as generally accepted accounting for purchases of life insurance.

In 1984, as new types of life insurance were introduced, the bulletin was reviewed. The AICPA's Accounting Standards Executive Committee reaffirmed support of the cash surrender value method in the October 1984 issues paper entitled, *Accounting for Key-Person Life Insurance.*

Under the Cash Surrender Value (CSV) method, premium payments are expensed and cash surrender value increases are reported as income.

Premium payment could be a one-time annual expense or may be amortized monthly over a period of one year. For example, if a premium were paid at the first of the year, a bank would credit cash and debit insurance expense. It also could credit cash and debit a prepaid insurance expense account and amortize the insurance expense monthly over the entire year.

A bank regularly receives a statement from its insurance carrier stating BOLI cash surrender value. This value may be reported as a credit to other income and a debit to the CSV asset account. In practice, the policy premium is often netted against the cash value increase to create net life insurance expense or income.

When an insured employee dies, the death proceeds from the policy are recorded as income and the accruals of cash value are reversed. Some banks use different account names in which they record income from increases in policy cash surrender values. These account names can include BOLI income, employee benefit income, tax exempt income, or other income.

In the following example, Bank X purchases a $200,000 single premium life insurance policy on an employee's life. At the end of year ten, the employee dies. The bank would make the following accounting entries.

SAMPLE INSURANCE ACCOUNTING ENTRIES

SINGLE EMPLOYEE DEATH ASSUMED
AT END OF YEAR TEN

Accounting Year	Insurance Expense (Premium)	Annual Cash Surrender Value Increase	Death Benefit	Net Life Insurance Income (Expense)	Balance Sheet Total (Cash Surrender Value)
1	($51,478)	$54,310	0	$2,832	$54,310
2	0	$2,824	0	$2,824	$57,134
3	0	$2,684	0	$2,684	$59,818
4	0	$2,808	0	$2,808	$62,626
5	0	$3,254	0	$3,254	$65,880
6	0	$3,322	0	$3,322	$69,202
7	0	$3,496	0	$3,496	$72,698
8	0	$3,674	0	$3,674	$76,372
9	0	$3,866	0	$3,866	$80,238
10	0	$4,054	0	$4,054	$84,292
Death	0	($84,292)	$200,000	$115,708	
	($51,478)	$0	$200,000	$148,522	$0

TAXATION OF BANK OWNED LIFE INSURANCE

Ignoring alternative minimum tax considerations, cash surrender value accumulations and death proceeds are not subject to income tax if policies are held until the deaths of insured persons. Conversely, premium payments are not deductible. In FASB 109, Accounting for Income Taxes, paragraph 14 specifies that the excess of cash surrender value of life insurance over premiums paid is a temporary difference if the cash surrender value is expected to be recovered by surrendering the policy. It is not a temporary difference if the asset is expected to be recovered without tax consequence upon the death of the insured.

Banks generally intend to hold insurance policies until the deaths of the insured, leaving policy income free of tax. If a bank were to change its intention, deferred taxes would be recorded for the temporary difference.

ALTERNATIVE MINIMUM TAX CONSIDERATIONS

Under regular tax rules, life insurance proceeds are excluded from gross income and, therefore, are income tax free to the beneficiary. Likewise, the inside buildup of life insurance cash value is excluded from gross income so long as it is left in the policy. A bank should calculate its taxes twice each year, once under the regular tax rules and once under Alternative Minimum Tax (AMT) rules. The bank then would pay taxes based on whichever calculation produces the higher tax amount.

To calculate its alternative minimum tax, a bank first calculates its alternative minimum taxable income (AMTI), which is regular taxable income with some adjustments and increases due to tax preference items such as accelerated depreciation. It also calculates its adjusted current earnings (ACE). The ACE adjustment is intended to reflect a corporation's pre-tax net book income as measured for financial accounting purposes. Its purpose is to ensure that a corporation, which reports a profit to the public or its shareholders, reports that profit to the IRS, as well. A bank or corporation must increase its AMTI by 75 percent of the amount by which ACE exceeds AMTI (or reduce its AMTI by 75 percent of the amount by which ACE falls short of AMTI).

Regulations set guidelines on the effect of BOLI on ACE. The income included in ACE differs depending on activity related to the insurance contract during the year. If a bank maintains the insurance contract and pays an annual premium, the income for ACE purposes for the year is calculated by taking the cash surrender value at the end of the year, minus the sum of the cash surrender value at the end of the prior year, plus the premiums paid during the year. This amount is reported as part of adjusted current earnings.

For example, if the cash surrender value at the end of year one were $12,000, at the end of year two $15,000, and the premium paid $2,500, the ACE income for year two would be $500 ($15,000-[$12,000+$2,500]). Calculations would change if there were death proceeds or distributions during the year.

While cash-value buildup and death proceeds affect the ACE adjustment, they do not necessarily subject the bank to AMT. Life insurance is only one of many factors that determine whether a bank must pay an AMT. However, it is possible that life insurance death benefits and cash-value increases, when added to other AMT preference items, could be enough to make a bank subject to AMT.

Any AMT tax paid may be carried forward for an unlimited period as a credit against taxes payable in future years under the regular tax calculation. Thus, AMT is not an additional tax, but rather a temporary tax that creates only a timing difference.

FINANCIAL STATEMENT DISCLOSURE

There is nothing in SEC Regulation S-X or GAAP that requires disclosure related to Bank-Owned Life Insurance. A bank may choose to disclose information about its other asset accounts at its discretion. Several recent annual reports from banks that had purchased life insurance included no disclosure about BOLI programs. Life insurance transactions are considered immaterial and do not require supportive information.

As banks increase purchases of insurance products, accounting issues will draw more attention. There may be increased demand for disclosure. The purchase of life insurance by a bank is a unique transaction and differs significantly from purchase of other kinds of assets.

Financial executives at banks that have purchased life insurance note that, in the beginning, accountants and bank auditors have to be walked through transactions in order to understand the activity. For most banks, ownership of life insurance is a new phenomenon. Many have not booked a death proceed.

In fact, life insurance provides significant benefits to a bank and involves simple accounting procedures. The value of BOLI's tax-favored treatment of cash buildup and death benefits, coupled with its utility as a funding source for employee benefit programs, makes the product very attractive. It promises a positive impact on the balance sheet, the income statement and, most importantly, shareholders.

CHAPTER 8
FEDERAL INCOME TAX ASPECTS OF BOLI

For a bank considering or owning BOLI, there are several key federal tax issues. Will the bank be eligible to exclude from current taxation the buildup in policy cash values ("tax-free inside buildup")? Will the bank be able to exclude from income the policy[1] death benefits? Will some aspect of the BOLI arrangement cause the bank to lose the ability to deduct interest that it pays? Other federal income tax issues that can arise (although not in the typical case) include the treatment of loans or distributions from BOLI policies prior to the death of the insured and the treatment of proceeds from the sale or exchange of policies. Additional considerations can arise in the case of variable life insurance contracts based on insurance company separate accounts.

While the reader probably already knows this, the lawyers have asked me to note that this discussion of selected federal income tax aspects of BOLI is intended only to provide an overview. It is neither an exhaustive discussion of

---

[1]The tax law tends to use the term "contract" to refer to a life insurance policy; the reader should generally view as interchangeable the terms "contract" and "policy" in the discussion below.

relevant federal (or state) tax law[2], nor a substitute for advice from a bank's own advisors who have considered the specific BOLI arrangement contemplated or undertaken by the bank. The IRS wants me to tell you that this book is not written to be, and cannot be, used by any person for the purpose of avoiding any penalties that may be imposed by the Internal Revenue Code ("Code"), or promoting, marketing or recommending any transaction or other matter discussed.

TAX-FREE INSIDE BUILDUP AND TAX-FREE DEATH BENEFITS

Generally, in order to qualify for tax-free inside buildup and the exclusion of death benefits, several tests must be satisfied, the most important of which is whether the policy meets the definition of "life insurance" for federal tax purposes. If a policy meets the definition of life insurance, the inside buildup is generally excluded from current taxation under Code section 7702(g) and the death benefits are generally excluded from income under Code section 101(a).

[2]For a detailed and lengthy discussion of the federal income tax treatment of life insurance, see, Zaritsky, Howard M. and Stephan R. Leimberg, *Tax Planning With Life Insurance*, Warren, Gorham & Lamont of RIA (2d ed. 2005).

Failure to satisfy these rules will subject policy income and death benefits to taxation.

DEFINITION OF LIFE INSURANCE

In order to be treated as a "life insurance contract" for federal income tax purposes, Code section 7702(a) requires that the contract or policy (1) be a "life insurance contract under applicable law"; and (2) either meet a cash-value accumulation test or meet guideline premium and cash-value corridor requirements. In addition, to constitute insurance, an arrangement must involve both "risk shifting" and "risk distribution."

LIFE INSURANCE CONTRACT UNDER APPLICABLE LAW —INSURABLE INTEREST

The tax laws do not specify what is meant by "applicable law," but it is generally understood that a life insurance contract must meet the laws of the state in which it is issued (and, in some cases the laws of the states in which the insured resides or the bank is domiciled, if these are not the states in which the policy is issued). Assuming that a

BOLI contract has been approved for sale by state regulators, the typical questions for a bank will be whether the bank has an "insurable interest" in the life of the insured employee under relevant state law and whether the bank has satisfied any applicable rules requiring notification of, and consent by, the insured. In many cases, a bank will have an insurable interest in the life of any individual who is an employee at the time first insured; in other cases, insurable interest may be limited to key and/or highly compensated employees. In some states, there is an insurable interest where insurance is purchased to fund an employer's obligations under employee benefit plans. A bank's insurable interest in an employee is not necessarily unlimited; state statutes or jurisprudence may limit the amount of policy coverage by reference to the employer's pecuniary interest in the life of the employee. In implementing any BOLI program, insurable interest should be verified under applicable state law.[3]

[3]A discussion of state insurable interest laws is beyond the scope of this chapter, but a generally up-to-date compilation of state insurable interest statutes can be found at http://www.deathandtaxes.com/insint.htm

CASH VALUE ACCUMULATION TEST/GUIDELINE PREMIUM—CASH VALUE CORRIDOR TESTS

A life insurance contract will satisfy the cash value accumulation test if, by the terms of the contract, the cash surrender value of the contract cannot at any time exceed the net single premium that would have to be paid at that time to fund future benefits under the contract.[4] Alternatively, a contract can satisfy the guideline premium and cash-value corridor tests. The guideline-premium test is satisfied if the sum of the premiums paid under a contract does not at any time exceed the guideline premium limitation as of such time.[5] The cash-value corridor test is satisfied if the contract's death benefit at any time is not less than a specified percentage of the contract's cash surrender value (the required percentage declines from 250 to 100 as the insured's age increases from 40 [or younger] to 95).[6] All three of these tests require complex actuarial calculations that can generally only be performed by the actuaries for the insurance company issuing the policy; the insurance company typically provides assurances that these tests will be satisfied.

[4]Code section 7702(b)(1).
[5]Code section 7702(c)(1).
[6]Code section 7702(d).

RISK SHIFTING/RISK DISTRIBUTION

Based on the U.S. Supreme Court's 1941 ruling in *Helvering v. LeGierse* (321 U.S. 531), an "insurance" contract must involve the shifting of economic risk of loss from the policyholder to the insurer and the distribution of that risk among the insurer's other policyholders. Risk shifting is not typically a concern in BOLI policies that have fixed cost of insurance charges with no "experience-rating" provisions. However, the issue of risk shifting should be considered carefully in policies with experience-rating provisions that seek to adjust the policy charges or premiums to reflect the actual mortality experience across a group of insured employees.[7] The requirement that a policy involve "risk distribution" among the various policyholders of an insurer is not typically a concern for BOLI, although issues could arise if the BOLI arrangement involves special-purpose

[7]In the context of pre-1996 leveraged COLI arrangements, several courts have found such arrangements to lack economic substance for federal income tax purposes, with the result that interest deductions were disallowed; these decisions turned in part on the "mortality neutrality" or experience rating provisions in the COLI arrangements. See, e.g., *Dow Chemical Company v. U.S.* (6th Cir., Jan. 23, 2006). Prior to these court decisions, it was generally understood (and even confirmed in Treasury Department Congressional testimony) that interest deductions were allowable under these leveraged COLI arrangements.

insurance entities doing limited business with parties other than the policyholding bank and its affiliates.

SPECIFIC RULES FOR COLI—CODE SECTION 101(J)

On August 17, 2006, a new provision, Code section 101(j), took effect for COLI (or BOLI) policies issued after that date.[8] The legislation generally conforms the statutory rules governing COLI to industry model uses today. In enacting the provision, lawmakers specifically sought to preserve the ability of companies to use COLI to meet critical needs, such as funding the cost of employee benefits and protecting against the loss of business owners or key employees. Under section 101(j), an employer's exclusion of death benefits from a COLI contract is generally limited to the amount of premiums paid by the employer unless the contract falls within certain specified exceptions and satisfies new notice and consent requirements. Contracts satisfying the notice and consent requirements *and* falling within one of the specified exceptions (generally designed to ensure that COLI is not taken out on rank-and-file workers) will continue to be

[8]Additional information about these COLI rules can be found at http://www.101j.com

eligible for exclusion of the full amount of death benefits. COLI contracts covered by the new legislation are also subject to reporting and record-maintenance requirements under new section 6039I.

NOTICE AND CONSENT REQUIREMENTS

The new notice and consent requirements are satisfied if, before the issuance of a COLI contract, the employee (A) is notified in writing that the employer intends to insure the employee's life and the notice sets forth the maximum face amount for which the employee could be insured at the time the contract was issued, (B) provides written consent to being insured under the contract and that such coverage may continue after the employee terminates employment, and (C) is informed in writing that the employer will be a beneficiary of any death benefits.

SPECIFIED EXCEPTIONS ALLOWING FULL EXCLUSION OF DEATH BENEFITS

Assuming that the above notice and consent requirements have been satisfied, if one of the following exceptions also applies, COLI contract death benefits will be eligible for exclusion from the employer's income:

- Directors and Highly Compensated Employees. Death benefits received in cases where the insured, at the time the contract was issued: was a director; was a 5-percent or greater owner of the business at any time during the preceding year; received compensation in excess of $95,000 (adjusted in the future for inflation) in the preceding year; was one of the five highest-paid officers; or was among the highest-paid 35 percent of all employees.
- Recent employee. Death benefits received in cases where the insured was an employee at any time during the 12-month period before his or her death.
- Death Benefits Paid to Insured's Heirs. Death benefits to the extent paid to a member of the family of the insured, an individual who is the designated beneficiary of the insured under the contract (other than the employer), a trust established for any such person, or the estate of the insured. This exception also includes death benefits used to purchase an

interest in the employer from any of the preceding persons.

REPORTING AND RECORD-MAINTENANCE REQUIREMENTS

Employers owning COLI contracts issued after August 17, 2006 are required to file a return with the IRS for each year the contracts are owned showing: (1) the number of employees at the end of the year; (2) the number of those employees insured under the COLI contracts; (3) the total amount of insurance in force under the COLI contracts; (4) the name, address, and taxpayer identification number of the employer and the employer's type of business; and (5) that the employer has a valid consent for each insured employee (or the number of insured employees for whom such consent was not obtained). Employers owning COLI contracts subject to these rules are also required to keep records necessary to determine whether the requirements of section 101(j) are met.

EFFECTIVE-DATE ISSUES

The new rules generally apply to COLI contracts issued after August 17, 2006. However, the new rules will not apply to a contract issued after that date pursuant to a section 1035 exchange for a contract issued on or before that date. For purposes of this effective-date rule, any material increase in the death benefit or other material change will cause the contract to be treated as a new contract (except that, with respect to a master contract, the addition of covered lives is treated as a new contract only with respect to the additional covered lives). A material increase in the death benefit that occurs as a result of the operation of section 7702 or the terms of the existing contract, provided that the insurer's consent to the increase is not required, will not cause a contract to be treated as a new contract. In addition, certain changes to a contract will not be considered material changes so as to cause the contract to be treated as a new contract, including administrative changes, changes from general to separate account, or changes as a result of the exercise of an option or right granted under the contract as originally issued. Even where a contract received pursuant to a section 1035 exchange is grandfathered from the section 101(j) rules, if the insured is no longer an employee at the time of the exchange, there may be significant adverse consequences for the employer as a result of section 264(f)'s pro rata interest disallowance (see discussion below).

SEPARATE ACCOUNT LIFE INSURANCE—INVESTOR CONTROL/DIVERSIFICATION ISSUES

For variable BOLI policies, particularly those based on separate accounts held by insurers, two separate but related questions arise involving prohibitions on "investor control" and requirements for "diversification." Failure to satisfy either of these rules could cause the policyholding bank to be treated as owning directly the investments funding the life insurance policies, with the result that the bank would be subject to current taxation on the investment income (dividends, interest, and gains) produced by those assets.

INVESTOR CONTROL

The "investor control" prohibitions arise out of IRS rulings starting in the late 1970's and are intended to carry out the tax policy goal that a taxpayer not be able to avoid tax on investments selected and controlled by the taxpayer merely by wrapping those investments in a life insurance policy. The typical BOLI arrangement allowing policyholders to allocate funds between several subaccounts having broadly defined investment strategies set by the insurance carrier is not likely to trigger investor-control concerns. However, policyholder rights to dictate or influence particular investments or the investment strategy of subaccounts, select or replace investment managers, and/or communicate with the investment managers of the subaccounts, could raise investor-control issues. Most insurance carriers have procedures in place intended to prevent arrangements from running afoul of the investor control prohibitions.

DIVERSIFICATION

In addition to the somewhat subjective "investor control" rules, Code section 817(h) specifically provides that variable life insurance contracts based on segregated asset accounts will not be treated as "life insurance" for tax purposes unless the contracts are adequately diversified. The Code and the tax regulations provide various safe harbors for meeting the diversification rules. Under one such safe harbor that is typically used, a contract will be considered adequately diversified if no more than 55 percent of the value of the total assets is represented by any one investment, no more than 70 percent by any two investments, no more than 80 percent by any three investments, and no more than 90 percent by any four investments. Because separate account life insurance policies are typically invested in a small number of special mutual funds created for such purposes, a key to satisfying the diversification rules is the ability to treat the life insurance contract as invested not in a particular mutual fund but instead in a pro rata share of the assets held by the mutual fund. The regulations generally permit this ability to "look through" the mutual fund (or a similar entity such as a real estate investment trust) in cases where (i) all of the beneficial interests in the mutual fund (or other entity) are held by one or more segregated asset accounts of one or more insurance companies, and (ii) public access to the mutual fund (or other entity) is available exclusively through the purchase of a variable contract.

ALTERNATIVE MINIMUM TAX

While a bank whose BOLI policies satisfy the foregoing will be eligible for tax-free inside buildup on those policies under the *regular* corporate income tax, the bank (unless eligible for a small corporation exception) will be required to take the policy inside buildup into account in computing the *corporate alternative minimum tax*.

INTEREST DEDUCTIONS

In past years much of the focus on interest deductions related to life insurance had to do with the treatment of interest paid on policy borrowings. Because of tax-law changes adopted in 1986 and 1996, interest deductions for policy borrowings are now severely constrained. More recently, the focus has been on rules adopted in 1997 that can cause a taxpayer to lose a deduction for a pro rata portion of its total interest expense, including for borrowings unrelated to life insurance policies. For a bank paying significant interest on deposits, it is important to ensure that these pro rata interest disallowance rules are not inadvertently triggered.

Interest Deduction Limitations

The applicable interest deduction rules are contained in Code section 264.

BORROWINGS TO PURCHASE OR CARRY SINGLE PREMIUM LIFE INSURANCE

Code section 264(a)(2) denies a deduction for interest on debt incurred or continued to purchase or carry a single premium life insurance contract. For this purpose, a life insurance contract is one where (1) substantially all of the premiums are paid within the first four years, or (2) an amount is deposited with the insurer for payment of a substantial number of future premiums. While many BOLI policies are single premium, this limitation is not likely to come into play unless the bank borrows against the BOLI policy or pledges the policy as collateral for an unrelated loan.

BORROWINGS TO PURCHASE OR CARRY INSURANCE OTHER THAN SINGLE PREMIUM LIFE INSURANCE.

Code section 264(a)(3) denies a deduction for interest on debt incurred or continued to purchase or carry a life insurance contract (other than one treated as a single premium contract, as discussed above) pursuant to a plan of purchase which contemplates the systematic or indirect borrowing of part or all of the increases in the cash value of the contract (from the insurer or otherwise). Exceptions to this rule are provided where no part of four of the annual premiums due during the first seven years is paid by means of indebtedness or where the indebtedness is incurred in connection with the taxpayer's trade or business. Because this rule reaches indirect borrowings and situations where the lender is not the insurance company, care must be taken that there is no planned linkage between a bank's borrowings and its payment of BOLI insurance premiums. However, in the typical case, a bank's borrowings will primarily consist of deposits, the amount and timing of which bear no relation to the BOLI plan.

OTHER POLICY BORROWINGS

As a result of 1996 law changes intended to prevent broad-based leveraged COLI arrangements, Code section 264 (a)(4) now generally provides a complete denial of deductions for interest on borrowings with respect to life insurance owned by the insured (i.e., policy borrowings). There is a limited exception for interest on up to $50,000 of indebtedness with respect to policies on a limited number (between 5 and 20) of key persons (i.e., officers and 20-percent owners). Because this exception is so limited, it is generally inadvisable for banks to borrow from BOLI policies.[9]

PRO RATA INTEREST DISALLOWANCE

As a result of 1997 law changes, Code section 264(f) provides that no deduction is allowed for the portion of the taxpayer's interest expense allocable to unborrowed policy cash values. While stated as a general rule, the core of this provision is in its exception for any policy owned by an

[9] This is particularly the case if the BOLI policies are modified endowment contracts (as discussed below) because the borrowings could be treated as taxable income.

entity engaged in a trade or business if the policy covers only one individual who, at the time first covered, is a 20-percent owner of the entity or an officer, director, or employee of the trade or business. This exception makes the provision inapplicable to typical BOLI policies taken out on the lives of a bank's officers or other employees. *However, there is a potential trap for the unwary* in the event a bank subsequently exchanges its original policy for another policy (even if the new policy is issued by the same insurance company that issued the original policy). While Code section 1035 typically prevents such an exchange from giving rise to taxable income, the policy received in the exchange will likely be seen as a new policy for purposes of section 264(f) and, if the insured employee is no longer an employee at the time of the exchange, will give rise to a disallowance of a portion of the bank's interest deductions. If the pro rata interest denial applies with respect to one or more contracts, the portion of the bank's total interest expense for which it will be denied a deduction is the ratio of its unborrowed policy cash values on applicable contracts to the sum of (1) its unborrowed policy cash values on all life insurance policies (and annuities and endowment contracts) and (2) the adjusted bases of other assets.

Simplified Example

As a simplified example of the section 264(f) pro rata disallowance rule where a bank exchanges its BOLI policies (including those on former employees), assume Bank has $10 billion of assets, $300 million of annual interest expense, and $200 million of life insurance cash value. Also assume that, at the time of the exchange, 65 percent of the insureds are no longer employees. After the exchange, Bank's annual interest expense deduction for tax purposes would be reduced by $3.9 million (($200 million of life insurance cash value/$10 billion of assets) x 65% former employees x $300 million annual interest expense). If the bank's tax rate is 35%, the interest expense disallowance results in an annual tax increase of $1.365 million, or a 0.68% reduction in the bank's yield on its BOLI policies; this tax will continue as long as the bank holds the policies and has interest expense.

ADDITIONAL TAX RULES

No Deduction for Premiums. Code section 264(a)(1) denies a deduction for premiums on a life insurance contract if the taxpayer is directly or indirectly a beneficiary of the contract. Thus, a bank will not be able to deduct its BOLI premiums.

Pre-Death Distributions. In general, policy distributions during the lifetime of the insured, including partial withdrawals which reduce policy benefits, are treated as tax-free until the policyholder has recovered all of its premiums (i.e., the policyholder's basis in the policy). Loans against the policy are not treated as distributions unless they remain on the policy when the policy is surrendered. Policy distributions in excess of the policyholder's basis are taxable up to the amount of accumulated income in the policy. However, substantially different rules apply in the case of policies that are modified endowment contracts (see discussion below). Because, in general, a bank will not take distributions from a BOLI policy during the insured's life, the treatment of pre-death distributions should not be a concern for most banks.

Modified Endowment Contracts. In order to limit the use of single-premium or rapidly funded life insurance, Congress enacted Code section 7702A which provides special tax treatment for modified endowment contracts (or

"MECs"). While MECs benefit from the same tax-free inside buildup and tax-free death benefits as other life insurance, special rules apply to policy distributions during the life of the insured that will cause such distributions to be taxable when they might not be taxable for other life insurance contracts. MECs are generally defined as contracts failing to meet a "7-pay test" – that is, where the accumulated amount paid under the contract at any time during the first seven years exceeds the sum of the net level premiums which would have been paid until then if the contract provided for paid-up future benefits after the payment of seven level annual premiums. If a contract is treated as a MEC, distributions (including policy loans, loans secured by the policy, interest accrued on a policy loan, withdrawals, cash dividends, and dividends retained by the insurer as principal or interest on a policy loan) are treated as ordinary income (up to the amount of gain in the policy) and are subject to an additional ten-percent excise tax. Again, because banks will not typically take distributions from BOLI policies prior to the insured's death, the MEC rules should not typically be a concern. However, the MEC rules should be carefully considered where a bank contemplates that it may need to tap into the policy values during the life of the insured (including pledging the policies as collateral for another loan).

***Caution*:** **MEC Aggregation Rules**. In applying the MEC rules, all MECs issued by the same insurance company to the same policyholder during a single calendar year are treated as a single MEC. Thus, distributions from a small number of policies can have a disproportionately large adverse tax consequence. For example, if the bank has two identical MEC BOLI policies (both acquired in the same year from the same insurer) on which it has paid a total of $200,000 of premiums, and the policies now have $400,000 of cash value, a borrowing of the cash value ($200,000) from one of the policies will give rise to ordinary income of $200,000 (i.e., the total build-up on both policies) plus a ten-percent penalty. As a result, in addition to the penalty, the bank will have gotten no benefit of tax-fee inside buildup from either of the policies.

Surrender or Sale of Life Insurance Contract. While death benefits may be tax-free, the amount realized on the surrender of a life insurance contract prior to the death of the insured will generally be ordinary income equal to the difference between the amount received by the taxpayer and the amount of the taxpayer's investment in the contract (typically the cumulative premiums paid less any prior non-taxable distributions). Sale of a life insurance contract to a third party will generally give rise to tax for the seller in the same manner as surrender of the contract to the insurer.

BOLI and Employee Benefit Plans. Banks may purchase BOLI in connection with various employee benefit programs, including as a means of offsetting the costs of those programs. For example, BOLI may be purchased in connection with qualified pension plans, nonqualified deferred compensation arrangements, or split-dollar life insurance arrangements. Extensive tax rules apply to the treatment of compensation, pension, and benefit arrangements (e.g., deferred compensation rules of Code sec. 409A). The tax treatment to the bank and its employees of various benefit programs should be discussed with a bank's advisors, but is beyond the scope of this book.

CHAPTER 9
ADMINISTRATION OF BOLI PLANS

A consultant can advise on the design and purchase of an effective BOLI plan. Similarly, a consultant can perform the equally important function of administering the plan.

The administration of BOLI encompasses the enrollment process, the initial policy delivery and plan review, and ongoing maintenance of the program. Many banks hire the same firms that helped design and purchase the plans to serve as program administrators.

A good administrator should have adequate computing systems and legal, actuarial and accounting expertise. The long-term viability of the consulting organization must also be considered. Most BOLI transactions are front-end loaded, which means most of the consultant's revenue comes in the early years of the plan. A consulting company should have procedures in place to ensure that sufficient revenue is gained from administration. Otherwise, the firm's viability depends on new sales.

The ideal consultant not only displays ingenuity in design, but also commitment to its administrative staff and systems. Administration should be an independent profit center not dependent upon further sales. Before a consultant is chosen, bank personnel should visit the candidate's administrative unit to inspect its operations and interview the people who would be involved in administering the BOLI plan.

ENROLLMENT

The first administrative step in BOLI is enrollment. Using an experienced consultant is advisable, particularly when multiple sites are involved. Although bank personnel will be involved in the enrollment process, a consultant provides manpower and expertise, prevents errors, and saves time and money.

An administrative consultant should begin by setting up a pre-enrollment planning meeting. The bank's human resources director, compliance officer, financial officer, and any other personnel who will be involved in enrollment should attend.

The enrollment plan should address the following:

- Consent of the insured
- Enrollment timing
- Corporate culture and perception of the plan
- Enrollment communication

Consent

The issue of the consent of insured employees is straightforward. Employees must be notified and consent to be insured.

Enrollment Timing

The bank determines the best policy date, taking into consideration fiscal year end, the timing of the premium payment, budget projection needs, and similar considerations. Once a date is set, the bank and the consultant construct an enrollment timeline. (See Appendix G for a typical BOLI implementation timetable.)

Corporate Culture

If an outside consultant is retained, the bank should inform the consultant about sensitivities in the employee population. For example, sometimes a simple word choice such as "officer," "employee," or "executive" can project an unintentional message. Heavy turnover, job cutbacks, reductions in benefits and similar factors should be considered as communications are developed in order to foster a positive perception of the plan.

Enrollment Communication

Giving prospective insured employees advance notice of the bank's request and an explanation of the bank's motivation can boost participation rates. In organizations that have implemented BOLI plans, over 95 percent of all eligible employees have voluntarily agreed to participate.

Communication about BOLI depends on which employees are included in the plan. An important concern is how best to communicate to employees about a plan that insures their lives, but does not provide them any death benefits. The answer is to emphasize that BOLI helps the employer offer competitive benefits.

Most BOLI plans are issued on a "Guaranteed Issue" basis, which means that all participants are included regardless of health as long as the human resources department certifies to the carrier that all insured participants are actively employed on the date of application, and have not missed more than five consecutive days in the last 90 days due to illness.

The introductory communication to employees is usually a one-page letter from a bank officer explaining the plan and its benefits. (See sample communication letters in Appendix H.) To help encourage enrollment, it is important to use bank colors and logos on enrollment materials and consent cards that match those used with other bank-sponsored plans. The consultant should review the design of the material, which must be approved by the bank and the insurance carrier. (See Appendix I for sample Consent Card).

Distribution and Collection System for Consent Cards

The appointment of site coordinators for each division or location improves accountability and, consequently, participation rates. In this method of distribution, each coordinator is mailed a package of enrollment materials and a census of eligible employees at his or her location. The coordinator is responsible for distributing the materials and collecting consent cards.

The bank gives the coordinator use of the interoffice mail system and schedules group or individual meetings. All locations should be instructed about any special methods to be used.

The site coordinators are responsible for auditing and reconciling the consent cards with the census. The coordinators then mail the cards back to a central location at the bank or consultant's office.

On receiving the cards, the consultant audits them for completeness and reconciles them with the original census of eligible employees. A report is prepared detailing the number of positive, negative, and no responses received. Based on this information the bank decides whether follow-up enrollments are necessary.

Policy Issue

Once enrollment is complete, the consultant organizes the completed cards and forwards them to the insurance carrier for processing. Policies are then issued by the insurance carrier and sent to the consultant. The consultant audits the policies for accuracy. Once the audit is completed and the necessary adjustments made, the policies are placed in the administrator's electronic data systems. An "as sold" financial analysis is run to compare the actual program to the version originally proposed. When this analysis is completed, the consultant schedules a meeting with the bank to deliver the policies and review the plan.

INITIAL ADMINISTRATION MEETING

An initial administration meeting should be scheduled soon after receipt of the policy contracts. This meeting should cover all bank concerns and establish a working relationship between the consultant and the bank's in-house administrative contact. The outside administrator should be informed about the bank's reporting requirements for the plan. The initial administration meeting usually covers the following topics:

Overview of the Plan

It is likely that some bank personnel who will be part of the internal administration of the plan were not involved in the bank's decision to purchase the BOLI plan. All involved parties should be briefed on the purpose and design of the plan, both short-term and long-term.

Policy Delivery

The policies are issued as one policy per life, or grouped together by age and sex, and issued on an aggregate basis. The bank should verify the terms of the policy contract by requesting a specimen policy from the carrier. The specimen is reviewed at the meeting. The bank's legal counsel also reviews the terms.

The policies themselves should be stored separately from personnel records of insured employees in order not to be mistaken for employee benefits. The location of the policies should be noted in an administration manual for future reference.

Review of Sample Reports

The consultant explains the types of reports that can be provided to help the bank manage the plan. These reports include cash values, death benefits, inventoried policies (on terminated insureds), deceased insureds, and other relevant material. The bank chooses which reports it wants and specifies how they should be customized.

Reporting Calendar

An important function of the initial administration meeting is to establish a timetable for reporting plan performance. Although there is a standard set of data that all BOLI purchasers need, the reports should be tailored based on such variables as organizational structure, the relationship of the policy date to the bank's fiscal year, the timing of the bank's budgeting cycle, and other bank requirements. It should be clearly established which bank staff member should receive each report.

Review of "As Sold" Illustration

An illustration detailing the financial impact of the plan is presented. This illustration projects the performance of the plan based on the specific lives insured, comparing the purchased plan with any previous illustrations presented during the marketing stage. Any variances must be explained.

Presentation of Administration Manual

The consultant provides the bank with an administration manual which:

- Documents the history and design of the BOLI plan, including policies issued, program design, population insured, assumptions used in the original financial analysis, and any other important information
- Specifies the reports needed by the bank and the reporting calendar
- Provides the administrator's name, address, and phone number
- Identifies a central location where the bank can store BOLI plan data
- Outlines procedures to be followed in case of death of insured employees

At the conclusion of this meeting, the bank's internal BOLI administrators should be familiar with the status of the plan. They should have a list detailing the delivery schedule for reports, identifying the individuals at the bank who will receive them. Bank staff members must know their contact person at the consultant's office for ongoing administrative issues and a backup person when the primary contact is unavailable.

MANAGEMENT REPORTS

Management reports for a BOLI program must be straightforward and easy to understand. As explained above, the bank agrees with the consultant on each report's due date and the identity of the bank staff member to whom each should be sent. Reports include:

Census Reconciliation

If the human resources department is responsible for enrollment, it uses this report to track consent agreements. The report lists which eligible employees gave consent, monitoring each one until policies are issued.

List of Comprehensive Policy Information

This list is an inventory of policies issued, including their initial premium and death benefit. The report is used as a benchmark.

Accounting Entries

These reports are provided to the appropriate accounting division on a schedule determined by the bank.

Premium Invoice

Most BOLI plan designs have a single invoice for the first policy year and no future billings. However, BOLI plans can have widely varying premium payment schedules. At a minimum, the invoice includes policy numbers, the names of insured employees, and premium amounts due.

Cash Surrender Values

The components of policy cash values are prepared for the bank on a scheduled basis. These reports provide information needed by the bank to properly book the insurance asset. The reports present information according to policy number. If the bank requires, the report provides subtotals by subsidiary.

Death Benefit Reports

The total death benefit amount for each policy, including its components, is prepared on a scheduled basis. Although death benefit amounts can change daily, the reports provide a rough idea of claim amounts when insured employees die.

Financial Projections

The projected financial impact of the plan on the bank should be prepared annually. This report projects performance of the plan for its remaining life. It illustrates changes in projected performance due to policy crediting rate changes or other changes.

Miscellaneous Reports

Other reports, such as insureds' beneficiary reports for the bank, reports on paid death benefits (if a death benefit is offered to the consenting insureds), and reports on deceased insureds or terminated insureds are prepared as needed.

PLAN TRANSACTION PROCESSING

The primary processing items in a BOLI plan are the initial premium invoice, death claims, and tracking of terminated insured employees.

Premium Invoice

Many BOLI plans have single premiums, although some carry multiple premiums. To preserve policy values as of a given date prior to final premium calculation, a bank may remit an estimated premium using a preliminary census. If consent of insureds is not needed, the estimate may coincide with the final premium. However, when consent is required, premium reconciliation is necessary when policies are issued. If the plan calls for multiple premiums, the bank is notified in advance of premium due dates and wire transfer instructions are given.

Death Claims

The consultant acts as an intermediary to expedite the processing of death claims. A typical death claim process begins when a bank notifies its consultant that a death has occurred in the insured population. The bank forwards a certified death certificate to the consultant. The consultant then prepares the appropriate documents, attaches the death certificate and forwards the material to the insurance carrier. If the insurance carrier requires additional information, it notifies the consultant.

Terminated Insureds

Since BOLI policies are generally kept in force on terminated employees, a bank must keep track of the post-termination status of former employees, the consultant contracts with a company that conducts Social Security sweeps and collects death benefit records from federal and state agencies. The consultant should alternate between two or more services since most get information from different sources and may have slightly different data. The consultant informs the bank of deaths of former employees and prepares necessary documents for the insurance carrier.

ANALYSIS SERVICES

At least once a year, a bank and its consultant should meet to review the performance of a BOLI plan. This analysis includes examination of historical plan performance against client objectives, as well as recommendations for reevaluation of strategy. It should encompass policy performance in dividends and interest, actual versus expected death claims experience, and corporate tax assumptions. When data indicates a strategy change, the consultant makes recommendations to the bank.

The best way to carry out the analysis is to use a reprojection system, which includes both insurance accounting and financial applications. A good reprojection system considers the entire BOLI product design, including the insurance carrier's rates, fees, interest and dividend history. These factors are measured against the parameters of each policy in the plan. This information is used to project financial values for each policy until maturity. The projections for each policy are combined to form a composite for the entire group.

Information on actual death claims, expected death claims, loans, withdrawals, and corporate tax rates is used to construct a variety of reports. These reports cover cash flow, profits and losses, and the performance of separate policy components. In addition, the internal rate of return of the entire BOLI plan is forecast. The bank must receive this information at least once a year to compare expected performance with actual results. The reprojection system should permit the bank to evaluate results on a quarterly or yearly basis.

VALIDATION OF VALUES AND RECORD KEEPING

The systems to validate and store carrier values are at the heart of proper plan administration. A consultant must be able to obtain current and projected values from the system so that a bank does not have to depend on the carrier for such information. Too often carriers make subtle mistakes in entering policies in their systems or in adding new data. Unless an independent source audits the values, mistakes can go undetected. In addition, the consultant should be able to generate customized reports that the carrier may not offer. These reports can include historical values, current values, and projected values. The items that should be tracked are:

- Policy cash values, broken into the appropriate components
- Policy death benefit, by components
- Premium paid
- Dividends paid
- Withdrawals and partial surrenders
- Death proceeds paid

Historical policy records are used in plan analysis to document trends in performance. Current values are used for accounting and management reports. Projected values are used for budget purposes and for analyzing expected performance.

TAX AND LEGAL CONSIDERATIONS

Periodically, tax and regulatory agencies revise their interpretations of the treatment of insurance and benefit plans. The bank must keep abreast of these changes in order to receive the most favorable tax treatment for its BOLI plan. A consultant normally tracks such changes, notifying the bank when appropriate.

DATA SYSTEMS

A BOLI plan represents a substantial investment for a bank. The plan uses confidential information, such as employee salary amounts. The values of the policies in the plan are also confidential and should be safeguarded. A consultant must store data on a secure system with appropriate backups and disaster-recovery procedures.

The software used to prepare reports should be customized so that a change in client strategy can easily be accommodated. Data systems fall into two categories: projection systems described above under "Analysis Services" and administrative systems. Administrative systems include information for each policy on premium payments, death benefit amounts, cash value amounts, death claims, loans, loan interest, withdrawals, and general information on the insured. This information can be transferred from the insurance carrier's system and modeled in ways not provided by the carrier. The consultant's system should be able to accommodate values from the insurance carrier at any point in the year, not just on an annual basis.

Although historical data generally should be kept separate from projected data, the reprojection system must be able to accept historical data on the BOLI plan for use in forecasting financial results. The reprojection system is used for financial reporting purposes separate from administrative requirements.

When possible, the bank should establish an electronic mail link with the consultant to facilitate communication. The consultant and bank can use their computer system to change routine information.

CHAPTER 10
THE REGULATORY ENVIRONMENT FOR BOLI

Regulatory guidance has evolved considerably since the first regulatory issuance to address BOLI, Banking Circular 249, was released in 1991. The most recent pronouncement, the Interagency Statement on the Purchase and Risk Management of Life Insurance (the Interagency Statement), was released in December 2004, and is significant in that it is the first time the four federal regulatory agencies have issued an interagency statement on the purchase of BOLI.

Before the Interagency Statement, federal regulatory guidance applied to national banks (OCC Bulletin 2000-23) or federally chartered thrifts (Regulatory Bulletin 32-16 from the Office of Thrift Supervision or "OTS"). It was often not clear how this prior federal guidance applied to state-chartered institutions, so several states issued their own guidance over the years. Generally, state-issued guidance closely followed prior federal guidance, but there are deviations. As a result, while the Interagency Statement is now applicable to all financial institutions, where state-issued guidance is *more restrictive* than the Interagency Statement, it must be followed by such state-chartered institutions. Only the Interagency Statement is discussed below.

INTERAGENCY GUIDANCE GENERALLY

The Interagency Statement provides that institutions "should have a comprehensive risk management process" for BOLI. That process should include:

- Effective senior management and board oversight;
- Comprehensive policies and procedures, including appropriate limits;
- A thorough pre-purchase analysis; and
- An effective ongoing monitoring and review system

Senior Management and Board Oversight. Regulators acknowledge that while the banking institution's board of directors may (and often does) delegate decision-making authority related to BOLI to senior management, the board remains ultimately responsible for ensuring that the purchase meets regulatory guidance.

Policies and Procedures. Each institution should establish internal policies and procedures governing its BOLI holdings, just as they have policies and procedures for investments or loans. An increasing number of institutions have adopted BOLI Policy Statements (see Appendix A), either on a stand-alone basis or incorporated into Investment Policy Statements. An effective BOLI policy statement should 1) address guidelines limiting the concentration of BOLI cash surrender values ("CSV") as compared to the bank's capital in the aggregate, as well as concentrations from any one insurance carrier; 2) lay out the due diligence that the institution will follow in purchasing BOLI, and; 3) establish a system for ongoing risk assessment, monitoring and review.

Concentration. Regulatory agencies have long suggested that an institution should not hold BOLI with CSV that, in the aggregate (from all insurance carriers), exceeds 25 percent of the institution's capital. For national banks, "capital" means Tier 1 capital plus Allowance for Loan and Lease Losses; for savings associations, it is total risk-based capital; and for state-chartered banks, it generally means Tier 1 capital.

Savings associations must get prior approval from the OTS to exceed the aggregate limit, while other institutions must seek prior approval from their boards of directors. An institution with BOLI holdings that exceed the established limit should expect closer scrutiny of the institution's policies and procedures, and be prepared to justify that the BOLI holdings above the aggregate limit are not an imprudent concentration of capital. All that said, at the time this book was written, numerous institutions held BOLI that exceeded the aggregate limit. While such a concentration may have received (and may continue to receive) notice in regulatory examination reports, this author is not aware of corrective action required for those institutions that have managed their BOLI appropriately.

In addition to the aggregate concentration limit, institutions should diversify their BOLI holdings and apply their legal lending limit to holdings with any one insurance carrier. This generally holds true whether the BOLI is general account or separate account.

An institution considering purchasing or reviewing existing BOLI should project its capital for 5-10 years and compare it to projected BOLI holdings. Caution is advised for those institutions whose capital is not expected to grow significantly relative to BOLI cash surrender values. For example, closely-held subchapter S-corporations that distribute a significant portion of their income in dividends may find that the growth in CSV will exceed the aggregate concentration limit rather quickly. Such institutions should consider whether lower internal limits are appropriate.

Pre-Purchase Analysis. The objective of a pre-purchase analysis is to help ensure that the institution's management understands the purpose and nature of the BOLI policies it is purchasing. A thorough documentation of the pre-purchase analysis process will help demonstrate that understanding to regulators. At a minimum, the Interagency Statement provides that the following steps should be included in a pre-purchase analysis.

I. <u>Identify the need for insurance, determine the economic benefit, and determine the appropriate insurance type</u>. Despite the investment features of BOLI, bank regulators have consistently stated that BOLI must not be purchased as an investment. While regulators have acknowledged four uses of BOLI, the vast majority of purchases are used to offset the costs of providing employee benefits; for example, pre- and post-retirement medical, qualified pension, 401(k) matches, nonqualified deferred compensation. An institution's analysis should indicate the intended use of its BOLI. Further, an institution should determine whether a general or separate account product would meet the identified needs.

II. Quantify the amount of insurance. Regardless of the internal limit that an institution adopts in its BOLI Policy Statement, it still must ensure that the BOLI purchase is not excessive in relation to the risk(s) to be insured. For example, where BOLI is used to offset the cost of employee benefits, an institution should compare the estimated present value of future after-tax costs of benefits to the present value of the expected cash flows from BOLI. Care must be taken to use reasonable assumptions.

III. Assess vendor qualifications. While BOLI may be purchased directly from the carrier or through a vendor, the vast majority of institutions use a vendor. In choosing a vendor, an institution should consider 1) its own knowledge of insurance risks; 2) the vendor's qualifications; and, 3) the amount of resources the institution is willing to expend to administer and service the BOLI.

A vendor's services may be critical to the successful

implementation and operation of a BOLI program. Factors that an institution should consider in selecting a vendor include 1) the vendor's ability to honor long-term commitments; 2) the adequacy of the vendor's services; and, 3) the vendor's reputation, experience, and financial soundness. For example, an institution could review audited financial statements of the vendor, visit the vendor's place of business, or inquire of trade associations. Further, the vendor's commitment to BOLI (measured in part by its investment in operational infrastructure necessary to support BOLI) is a "key consideration" in vendor selection.

Despite the invaluable role that a qualified vendor can play, the Interagency Statement cautions that management, and not just the vendor, must demonstrate a familiarity with the technical details of, and be able to explain the rationale for, the BOLI the institution holds. The Interagency Statement admonishes that reliance solely upon pre-packaged, vendor-supplied compliance information "does *not* demonstrate prudence," and an institution should maintain its own notes and records of its pre-purchase analysis.

IV. Review characteristics of available products. An institution should review the myriad design features of BOLI, including 1) whether a general account, separate account, or hybrid product is appropriate; 2) whether a Modified Endowment Contract (MEC) or non-MEC is desired (see Chapter 8 on Federal Income Tax Aspects of BOLI for an explanation of MEC); and 3) the method used to credit earnings. These are discussed further below.

V. Select carrier. For the banking institution to be entitled to anticipated tax benefits, BOLI policies must be held until the insured dies. As a result, the institution will be entering into a long-term (perhaps 40 years or more) commitment — carrier selection is one of the most critical decisions in a BOLI purchase. The Interagency Statement suggests conducting a credit analysis on the selected carrier(s) as an institution would in commercial lending situations.

In addition to credit quality, which presumes a review of various credit ratings, an institution should also consider a carrier's:

- Commitment to BOLI. For example, has the carrier been consistently in the BOLI market, or just recently developed a BOLI product? If the latter, appropriate inquiry should be undertaken to ensure the long-term commitment of the carrier. Carriers without such market commitment may have an incentive to lower the interest-crediting rate, thereby reducing the economics of their product;
- General reputation;
- Experience in the marketplace; and
- Past performance.

While an institution can change from one carrier to another in a tax-free exchange under Internal Revenue Code §1035 (see Chapter 8), there may be significant constraints. For example, it is generally understood that insurable interest must be present at the time of such an exchange; if the insured has left the employ of the institution, in most states insurable interest will not be present. Further, the original carrier may impose an exchange fee or market value adjustment, reducing the CSV available for transfer; this fee or adjustment may have an impact on the institution's balance sheet.

VI. <u>Determine the reasonableness of compensation under split-dollar life insurance arrangements</u>. In addition to providing an efficient means of financing employee benefits, BOLI can be used to supplement life insurance benefits for insured employees. When done through a split-dollar arrangement, federal income tax regulations require the participant to recognize the economic value of the life insurance benefit. The regulations provide a means for measuring that value, referred to as "imputed income." An institution considering a split-dollar life insurance arrangement should include the imputed income from such an arrangement in its determination of the total compensation it provides to the participant, and ensure that the total compensation is not excessive. Note that shareholders who are not officers, directors, or employees of an institution should not participate in a split-dollar life insurance program, as they should not receive compensation, as opposed to dividends, from the institution.

VII. Analyze the risks of BOLI and ability to monitor and respond to them. The risks of BOLI (see below) should be thoroughly evaluated, as well as the institution's ability to identify, measure, monitor, and control them.

VIII. Evaluate alternatives. Despite the apparent advantages of BOLI, an institution should compare BOLI to alternative methods for financing employee benefits, including the cost of doing nothing.

IX. Document decision. For each of the steps above, an institution should maintain appropriate documentation of its findings. In addition, a BOLI Policy Statement and annual reports from ongoing review/monitoring should be readily available for review and consultation.

Ongoing Monitoring/Review. Given the very long-term nature of a BOLI program, ongoing assessment can be as critical to the success of the program as the initial pre-purchase analysis. Changes in tax laws, or in the financial condition or BOLI commitment of the carrier, can have a significant adverse impact for the unwary. The Interagency Statement suggests a board-level review at least annually, covering—at a minimum—the following: Re-assessment of the risks (discussed below);

- Identification of which employees are, or will be, insured; for example, vice presidents and above, employees of a certain grade level;
- Assessment of the death benefit amounts relative to employee compensation;
- Calculation of the percentage of insureds still employed by the institution;
- Evaluation of the material changes to BOLI risk-management policies;
- Assessment of the effects of policy exchanges, if any;
- Analysis of the mortality performance and impact on income;
- Evaluation of material findings from internal and external audits and independent risk-management reviews;
- Identification of the reason for, and tax implications

of, any policy surrenders, and;

- Peer analysis of BOLI holdings.

RISKS OF BOLI

Regulators have identified eight areas of risk for BOLI.

I. Liquidity. Liquidity is the risk to the institution's earnings and capital arising from the inability to meet obligations when they come due without incurring unacceptable losses. Even though BOLI can be surrendered for cash with relative ease, it is a long-term, illiquid asset in banking parlance. The economics of BOLI work best when the policy is held until the death of the insured, and a surrender of the policy before death would cause taxation of the policy's CSV gains. Since current accounting guidance does not require accruing any deferred tax liability for potential future surrenders of BOLI, an early policy exit could produce adverse financial consequences, thus compromising the success of the BOLI program. The illiquidity of BOLI, together with the difficulty of projecting an institution's liquidity needs far into the future, is a driving force behind adhering to concentration limits of CSV.

II. Transactional/Operational. Transactional/operational risks arise from an institution's failure to fully understand or to properly implement a transaction. For example, not fully understanding a product's surrender costs could result in accounting treatment that is far different than anticipated. To mitigate this risk, management should understand the variables that dictate the product's performance, such as interest crediting rates, mortality costs, and other expense charges. In addition, separate account products typically involve third parties, such as investment managers and stable value providers, and management needs to consider this added complexity. Finally, failure to comply with the tax requirements enacted in 2006 could have a significant adverse impact on program performance. See Chapter 8 for a further discussion of Internal Revenue Code section 101(j).

III. Tax and Insurable Interest. As mentioned previously, the economics of a BOLI program will depend, in part, on the tax treatment of policy proceeds. Under current law, when a policy is held until the death of the insured, the death benefits are generally free of federal income tax. See Chapter 8 for a further discussion of the tax implications.

To have a valid insurance contract, an institution must first have an insurable interest in the person to be insured. Insurable interest is a function of state law (a discussion of each state's insurable interest laws is beyond the scope of this book). Some states have statutes that explicitly give an employer an insurable interest in its employees, while other states have jurisprudence that provides such an insurable interest. Still other states have little or no guidance on whether an employer has an insurable interest in the life of an employee. Regardless of where an institution is domiciled, the consensus approach, which has been supported by recent high-profile court cases, is to follow the insurable interest requirements of the state in which the proposed insured is a resident.

Even where valid insurable interest exists under state law, federal income tax law imposes some notice and consent requirements when insuring employees and directors in order to achieve the intended tax benefits. See Chapter 8 for further discussion.

It is critical to understand that without a valid insurable interest, there will likely be unfavorable tax treatment of the BOLI. The inside build-up of CSV as well as the policy's death proceeds would be taxed. Furthermore, the "rightful beneficiaries" of the insureds could have claims against the institution for the death proceeds. The Interagency Statement cautions institutions to have appropriate legal review to help ensure compliance with insurable interest requirements.

IV. Reputation. Reputational risk arises from potential negative publicity regarding an institution's business practices. In the case of BOLI, it could arise from any negative perceptions associated with an employer benefiting from life insurance on employees. This risk can be greatly mitigated by providing adequate notice and disclosure to potential insureds, and getting their written consent to be insured by the institution, even if such notice and consent are not required to satisfy state insurable interest laws. Indeed, the success of the program may hinge on following appropriate notice and consent requirements under the Internal Revenue Code section 101(j), discussed above. Further, an institution should monitor how much insurance it purchases on any one individual, and take steps to ensure the amount is reasonable.

V. Credit. Credit risk arises from an obligor's failure to meet the terms of any contract. With general account BOLI, the carrier assumes the default risk of any individual asset in its portfolio, while the institution assumes the default risk of the carrier. Given the very long-term nature of BOLI, the financial soundness of the underlying carrier becomes important. Driven by this marketplace concern, the predominant carriers that provide general account BOLI are typically among the "highly" and "very highly" rated companies in the insurance industry.

With separate account BOLI, the carrier risk is mitigated since the institution generally assumes the default risk of any individual investment while the carrier continues to provide death benefit promises. To provide for consistent cash value treatment, as opposed to daily fluctuations in the value of the underlying separate account assets, a stable value wrapper is often used with separate account BOLI. Since the stable value provider assumes some or all of the market risk, this provider should be given the same credit consideration as a general account carrier.

VI. Interest rate. Interest rate risk arises from movements in interest rates. For BOLI, it is primarily associated with the maturities of assets in an underlying investment portfolio. For general account BOLI, the typical carrier invests predominantly in high-quality bonds, with an average duration of 4-8 years. For separate account BOLI, each particular subaccount has a stated objective; for example, mirroring the carrier's general account, mortgage-backed securities, or U.S. Treasuries. It is important that an institution understand how a particular carrier or separate account will approach investments, and to monitor the carrier for any changes.

VII. Compliance/Legal. Compliance/legal risks arise from potential violations of statutes, rulings, regulations, etc. Failure to comply with such laws can jeopardize the success of a BOLI program. For example, failing to have proper insurable interest in an insured could cause a loss of tax benefits, expose the institution to reputation risk, and result in litigation brought by the insured's natural beneficiaries. Further, splitting of commissions between the vendor and the institution (or one of its affiliates) may violate state anti-rebating laws, and may result in fines or suspension of the institution's license to do insurance business. The Interagency Statement cautions that institutions should seek advice of counsel on these issues.

VIII. Price. Price risk arises from changes in the value of the underlying assets. It typically does not exist in general account BOLI, since the carrier assumes asset default and market value risk. However, it is present with separate account BOLI, since the institution assumes default risk of all underlying assets. To mitigate or even eliminate daily fluctuations in CSV, most separate account BOLI have a stable value wrapper. It is important to note that the wrap provider protects only against declines in the underlying asset value, not against any default with respect to those assets.

RISK-BASED CAPITAL TREATMENT

One of the more noteworthy changes in the Interagency Statement from prior guidance is a unified approach to the risk-based capital treatment of BOLI. General account BOLI has always received, and will continue to receive, a 100-percent risk weight.

Separate account BOLI is generally eligible for one of two "look through" approaches, under which an institution may apply the risk weights of the underlying separate account assets to determine a total risk-based weighting for its BOLI. It is important to note that regardless of the underlying asset, the separate account risk weight cannot be less than 20 percent. Furthermore, the elements of separate account BOLI that represent general account-like claims, such as DAC and mortality reserves and stable value protection, will always receive a 100-percent risk weight.

OTHER DEVELOPMENTS

BOLI continues to evolve quickly, especially for separate account products. Recently, interagency guidance was issued that allowed a specialized separate account to qualify for Community Reinvestment Act (CRA) credit. (See OCC Interpretive Letter 1008, October 2004.) While this potential CRA credit is appealing, as a practical matter, the transaction would have to be large enough, and the institution would have to be in a sufficiently large geographic/metropolitan area, for sufficient assets to be available to be put into the separate account; such a condition will result in potential CRA benefit to relatively few institutions.

SUMMARY

BOLI guidance has evolved significantly over the years, with each new update reflecting an increasing understanding of BOLI by the regulators. While regulatory cautions regarding BOLI are valid, with effective policies and procedures, consultation and sound guidance, an institution should find that implementing a BOLI program is generally not that difficult. The key to a successful program is documentation, documentation, documentation.

CHAPTER 11
Partnering For Success: How To Choose A Consultant

THE NEED FOR A CONSULTANT

A BOLI plan is complex. There are many aspects that require expert attention. Optimal execution requires expertise in a number of different areas. A good consultant will provide the necessary expertise.

> Developing this knowledge base requires resources and time. Unless a bank is willing to develop its own expertise, the only viable alternative is to purchase these services. With a transaction of the size and importance of a BOLI plan, a reliable and highly regarded consulting firm is needed.

Another important reason for choosing a consultant is to obtain leverage in carrier relationships. Although carriers value client relationships, they do not work for a bank. Carriers are selling products. Their goal is to maximize profits while maintaining a competitive edge. Even the competitive advantage gained through product performance is less important to carriers than maintaining their industry ratings. Ratings are their lifeblood and an important competitive advantage. Insurance carriers have complete latitude in determining the competitiveness of their products. At any time, they can increase their spreads and lower a bank's yields.

THE ROLE OF THE CONSULTANT

Understanding the role of the consultant is important in order to make a proper selection. Generally, a BOLI consultant can be an agent of a single insurance company (a "captive agent"), an agent of multiple insurance companies (a "non-exclusive" agent) or a broker. It is important to distinguish between the various types of consultants in the selection process. It will help identify those BOLI consultants who have access to a full range of products and a variety of carriers. Making the right choice is critical in order to get access to objective information and the best product lines, pricing components, and investment performance.

THE CONSULTANT AS MEDIATOR

The role of a consultant is to build a communication bridge between a bank and an insurance company, which will serve as a pathway for the flow of information among all parties in the transaction—the bank, the carrier, and the consultant. The skill of a BOLI consultant will determine how much and what kind of information is available, and how fast it can be obtained. Key to this role is a consultant's knowledge of carriers and their products.

An experienced consultant works with carriers to help them respond to changes in the market. A consultant advises insurance companies on how to update existing products, make pricing more competitive, develop new products, and add plan features which respond to market needs. A top-notch firm is an innovator that designs new products. A consultant's design capabilities should be at least as good as, if not better than, the technical or creative capacities of carriers. A consultant's understanding of every BOLI component must be comprehensive.

THE CONSULTANT AS NEGOTIATOR

With an insider's knowledge about how carriers and products work, a consultant is well positioned to negotiate a BOLI transaction on behalf of a bank. This knowledge includes policy pricing, underwriting, insurable interest, contractual provisions, future product availability, and competitive performance in the short- and long-term.

THE CONSULTANT AS BOLI PLAN ADMINSTRATOR

After a BOLI plan is set up, a consultant can administer the policies, providing management services over the life of the plan. (The administration of BOLI is detailed in Chapter 9.) A BOLI program may continue 40 years or longer. A bank should select a qualified, experienced consultant with whom it can comfortably work over a long period of time.

In essence, a consultant is a bank's "plan insurance" for successful and timely delivery of the purchased product. The complexity of the transaction requires attention to intricate details, ensuring the carrier delivers a plan that conforms to previous agreements.

DIRECT PURCHASES

Occasionally, a prospective buyer may consider purchasing BOLI directly from an insurance company. Sometimes bank officials believe their institutions will benefit by eliminating a consultant's role.

Going direct is not necessarily a viable option with many insurance companies. Many carriers distribute their products only through consultants, preferring to be relieved of all tasks, except delivering the best product. Insurance companies recognize that, more than just selling or placing a product, BOLI involves a partnership. The best way they can participate successfully in a partnership is by working with experienced consultants.

Astute carriers also know that consultants can help them compete better in the market. That ability translates into better products for buyers.

A third reason carriers choose to work through consultants is to improve policy administration. A consultant will work with a carrier to service policies, acting as a check point for possible errors and oversights. A consultant ensures accuracy, and provides superior long-term plan administration.

Still, some carriers have tried to market products directly to buyers. Their efforts have not met with much success because the product itself is only a part of a BOLI transaction. For companies that have tried to sell direct, the inexperience of their sales forces and home offices has translated into high marketing and sales costs that are ultimately passed on to buyers.

A survey of the market shows that few major BOLI plans have been transacted on a direct basis. The most prudent banks select a top-rated consultant group with which to work. Going direct can mean sacrificing competitive position, negotiating leverage, and long-term plan performance.

Lower Cost: Retail vs. Wholesale

All the same, some buyers believe it may be cheaper to buy BOLI directly from carriers. They believe a better deal can be had if they cut out the middleman, the broker/ consultant, and buy wholesale, directly from the carrier.

Product placement represents a cost that carriers build into policy expenses loads. One way or another, a carrier will seek to recover the expense. Product administration is another expense that carriers build into policy loads. These costs do not disappear when a consultant is eliminated. Depending on experience and internal administration, a consultant performs these services more efficiently and accurately than a carrier.

The carriers in the BOLI market are AAA and AA+ rated with billion dollar asset bases. Their financial position and claims-paying ability are based on their success in investing prudently. An insurance company's business is to minimize risk, cover its expenses, create profits, and maintain or increase its ratings. As single customers, most banks have neither the knowledge nor influence to negotiate the best margins in a direct purchase.

WHAT TO LOOK FOR IN A CONSULTANT

The role of a consultant is to put together the most profitable and financially sound BOLI program possible. A consultant should be selected with care since a bank will work with the firm for years to come.

Criteria for selecting a BOLI consultant include:

- Experience in the market
- Management stability
- Product availability
- In-house administrative capability and technical resources
- Design capability
- Impartiality

A buyer should evaluate a consultant informally through meetings and references, and formally through a "Request for Proposal."

Experience and Stability

Experience is a function of how long a company has been in business, and the growth of its client base and support staff. A buyer should look for evidence that a consultant is willing to grow and change as the market changes.

A bank should ensure that a consultant has specific expertise in BOLI. There are many different focuses in the life insurance industry. A successful consultant in individual sales and personal financial planning would be ill-equipped to help a bank carry out a large life insurance purchase.

A consultant's capabilities are demonstrated by his track record with carriers and clients.

A consultant must also understand the regulatory environment, taking into account rules enforced by a variety of public agencies and adhering to legal and insurance company guidelines on insurable interest. A well-regarded BOLI consultant may help official agencies develop guidelines and tools of analysis.

Stability and staying power are essential in a consulting firm. As it implements a BOLI plan, a bank invests time and resources building a relationship with its consultant. This investment should be protected by working only with a consulting firm that is likely to be around for a long time.

A consulting firm should have a realistic succession plan for key personnel. If a firm is built around one or two individuals whose leadership for continuing the business, a bank could be vulnerable. A responsible consulting firm thinks and acts for the long term.

A consulting firm must also have adequate financial resources. Profitability helps ensure a firm's staying power if profits are reinvested in the business to develop resources, recruit and train top talent, and provide state-of-the-art tools. Such investments are evidence that a firm is planning to be around for a long time.

A client may ask to see a consulting firm's audited financial statements. Such statements show whether a firm is well capitalized or straining under a heavy burden.

Product Availability

There are more buyers than ready and willing suppliers in the BOLI market. As a result, product availability does not meet demand and requires negotiation with carriers. In some instances, product may be reserved for certain consultants based on the ability of those firms to place product quickly and to complete financially sound transactions. A top-notch consulting firm not only seeks out products for buyers, but also uses its own resources to design new products for the market. A firm's ability to innovate establishes it as a leading edge consultant from the viewpoint of carriers and prospective buyers.

Administrative Capabilities

The administrative capabilities of a firm are vital to the long-term success of a BOLI plan. The administrative services a firm provides, and the data systems it maintains, are important buyer concerns. A consultant should not rely on carriers for reporting functions, but should work independently to provide accurate, high-quality information to clients. Administrative calendars should be tailored to banks' reporting needs. Responsiveness and timeliness go hand-in-hand with accuracy.

A consultant's administrative abilities can be checked by determining the number of policies the firm has under administration and obtaining references from other clients across such disciplines as finance and human resources. The best way to learn whether a consultant is a good administrator is to visit the firm's administrative facility, and meet staff people who will work with the BOLI plan on a daily basis.

In-House Resources

A quality firm should be able to offer clients the services of staff attorneys, accountants, actuaries, product designers, benefit experts and communication specialists.

Design Capabilities

Product knowledge is an absolute essential in a consultant. A consultant should be prepared to custom-design products and tailor plan features to meet a bank's specific needs.

Impartiality

Only an impartial firm can truly serve a bank as a partner. Some consultants have entered into arrangements with carriers in which they receive a share of profits from business they place for the carrier. This type of arrangement is not disclosed to the buyer, but can represent a significant part of a broker's income. Such hidden compensation is not an acceptable payment arrangement as it violates industry standards and good business practice.

PARTNERING FOR SUCCESS

An impartial and objective consultant will help a bank develop a BOLI plan that properly serves all parties, meeting the financial criteria of the buyer, providing fair compensation to the consultant, and profitable business to the insurance company.

By carefully selecting a BOLI consultant, a bank can lay the foundation for a successful plan. Bank officials should seek a consulting firm they trust and with which they can work comfortably.

APPENDICES

APPENDIX A
BANK-OWNED LIFE INSURANCE (BOLI) POLICY STATEMENT

I. PURPOSE

The purpose of this policy statement is to outline the Institution's practices for purchasing and holding bank-owned life insurance ("BOLI"). The fundamental elements of our BOLI statement include Board and Senior Management oversight of purchasing practices and a comprehensive risk-management process that effectively identifies, measures, monitors, and controls risk. These risks include, but are not necessarily limited to: liquidity risk, transactional/operational risk, reputation risk, credit risk, interest rate risk, compliance/ legal risk and price risk. Both the Board and Management believe that effective management of the risks associated with BOLI represents an essential component of safe and sound banking practices.

II. SCOPE

Except for the Pre-Purchase Analysis in section B1, this policy statement applies to all BOLI contracts held by the Institution regardless of when acquired. The Pre-Purchase Analysis in B1 applies to BOLI purchased after December 7, 2004.

III. BOARD AND SENIOR MANAGEMENT OVERSIGHT

In addition to conducting a risk assessment as part of a thorough pre-purchase analysis, monitoring BOLI risks on an ongoing basis is an essential component of safe-and-sound practices. Management will review the performance of the Institution's insurance assets with the Board at least annually. More frequent reviews are appropriate if there are significant anticipated changes to the BOLI program. Management is responsible for complying with the guidance and limits set forth in this policy statement, but the Board must understand the complex risk characteristics of the Institution's insurance holdings and the role the assets are intended to play in the Institution's overall business strategy. Although the Board may delegate decision-making authority related to BOLI purchases to senior Management, the Board remains ultimately responsible for ensuring that the purchase and holding of BOLI is consistent with safe and sound banking practices.

IV. RISK MANAGEMENT PROCESS

The Institution's risk management process for BOLI includes a series of policies, procedures and limits for conducting pre-purchase and ongoing analyses.

A. Policies, Procedures and Limits

The policies described herein are based upon our objective, which includes the desire to recover costs associated with providing employee, and, if applicable, director benefits.

A.1. Limits

The Institution will estimate the size of the obligation or the risk of loss to ensure that the amount of BOLI purchased is not excessive in relation to the estimate. The estimate of the amount of insurance needed will be based on reasonable financial and actuarial assumptions. Management will be responsible for providing support, with objective evidence, of the reasonableness of all assumptions used in determining the appropriate amount of insurance coverage needed by the Institution, including the rationale for the discount rates and cost projections.

Provided such purchases of BOLI are conducted in accordance with this Policy Statement, Management shall have authority to acquire new or additional BOLI such that the Institution's aggregate cash surrender value ("CSV") of BOLI from all insurance companies generally shall not exceed ________________ percent (___ %) of the Institution's capital. In addition, the aggregate CSV of policies from any one insurance carrier generally shall not exceed ___________ percent (___ %) of the Institution's capital. Also, the net amount of insurance on any one individual may not exceed _______________ (___) times the individual's total annualized compensation at the date of purchase without prior Board approval. Furthermore, BOLI may only be purchased on employees in the top thirty-five percent (35%), measured by compensation, or on Directors of the Institution; purchases on employees of a subsidiary or the holding company of the Institution must be specifically approved by the Board. Management will take two specific actions if the Institution plans to acquire BOLI in excess of, or if BOLI CSV grows in excess of, the capital concentration thresholds listed above. First, Management will conduct an analysis to support that such acquisitions or growth do not rise to an imprudent capital concentration. Second, Management will obtain approval from the Board or a designated Board committee prior to the acquisition or retention. The Board or designated Board Committee will carefully consider Management's analysis prior to acquiring or retaining BOLI in excess of these limits. As part of this analysis, Management will inform the Board of the interagency statement, remind them of the illiquid nature of the insurance asset, advise them of the potential adverse financial impact of early surrender, and identify any other significant risks associated with BOLI.

B. Risk Management

Management will ensure that it identifies and measures the risks associated with BOLI purchases prior to acquisition and annually after purchase.

B.1 Pre-Purchase Analysis

Management will conduct a pre-purchase analysis. Consistent with the interagency statement issued by the Office of the Comptroller of the Currency (OCC Bulletin 2004-56), the Board of Governors of the Federal Reserve System (SR 04-19), the Federal Deposit Insurance Corporation (FIL-127-2004), and the Office of Thrift Supervision (TB 84), (collectively, the "Interagency Statement"), such analysis shall consider the following:

1. Identification of the need for insurance and determination of the economic benefits and appropriate insurance type;
2. Quantification of the amount of insurance appropriate for the Institution's objectives;
3. Assessment of vendor qualifications (see Section B.5);
4. Review of characteristics of the available insurance products;
5. Selection of the carrier(s) (see Section B.3);
6. Determination of the reasonableness of compensation provided to the insured employee if the insurance results in additional compensation;
7. Analysis of the associate risks and the ability to monitor and respond to those risks (see below);
8. Evaluation of alternatives;
9. Documentation of decision.

B.2 Ongoing Risk-Management Process

Subsequent to purchase, Management will conduct an analysis and report to the Board annually. More frequent reviews will be performed if there are significant changes or anticipated changes to the BOLI program (such as additional purchases, a decline in the financial condition of a carrier, anticipated policy surrenders, or changes in tax laws that could have an impact on the performance of BOLI). Consistent with the Interagency Statement, such ongoing annual analysis shall consider the following:

1. Assessment of liquidity risk, transactional/ operational risk, tax and insurable interest implications, reputation risk, credit risk, interest rate risk, compliance/legal risk, and price risk;
2. Identification of which employees are, or will be, insured;
3. Assessment of death benefit amounts relative to employee salaries;
4. Calculation of the percentage of insured persons still employed by the Institution;
5. Evaluation of the material changes to BOLI risk-management policies;
6. Assessment of the effects of policy exchanges;
7. Analysis of mortality performance and impact on income;
8. Evaluation of material findings from internal and external audits and independent risk-management

review;

9. Identification of the reason for, and tax implications of, any policy surrenders; and
10. Peer analysis of BOLI holdings.

B.3 Carrier Selection, Retention and Credit Risk

The Institution will perform a credit analysis on the selected carrier(s) in a manner consistent with safe-and-sound banking practices for commercial lending, including seeking input from the Institution's credit risk-management function where appropriate. Management will review the product design, pricing, and administrative services of the proposed carriers, and compare them with the Institution's needs. Management will also be responsible for reviewing the carrier's commitment to the BOLI product, as well as its credit ratings, general reputation, experience in the marketplace and past performance.

The Institution's exposure is managed by the use of highly rated carriers and by diversification among those carriers. This policy statement limits the Institution's exposure to any one carrier and to BOLI overall, unless there is specific Board approval otherwise.

The Institution will only enter into BOLI arrangements with carriers who meet the minimum ratings from two of the three following rating agencies: A- from A.M Best, A- from Standard & Poor's, or A3 from Moody's. Furthermore, the carrier's investment portfolio should contain less than 10% equities. The Institution will conduct an annual credit analysis for all existing carriers. If a separate account product is purchased, only bank-eligible investments may be owned within the BOLI subaccount(s), unless the BOLI will be used to informally finance the Institution's equity-linked deferred-compensation liabilities.

Internal Revenue Code Section 1035 permits a policyowner to transfer, on a tax-free basis, policies from Carrier "A" to Carrier "B." There are special interest disallowance provisions with respect to exchanging policies on the lives of former employees. Further, certain carriers may impose charges or other provisions in the event a 1035 exchange is invoked. The Institution will consider surrendering the policies or invoking a 1035 exchange if any of the following events occur:

- Ratings change. The Institution will put "on watch" any carrier that has its rating dropped (i) by two rating agencies or (ii) by two levels by any one rating agency. The Institution will monitor the financial conditions of such a carrier regularly and will conduct a credit analysis quarterly until the credit rating is restored. Management will evaluate, monitor and compare the situation to the carrier's "peers." The Institution shall surrender the applicable policies or invoke a 1035 exchange if the existing carrier's rating falls below any of the following ratings: B from A.M Best, BBB- from Standard & Poor's, or Baa3 from Moody's.
- Policy yields. If the BOLI from a given carrier lags behind the carrier's peer group, Management will evaluate the reasons and compare such BOLI to its "peer products," considering first-year and renewal

rates on a current and historical basis.

- Carrier exits market. If the insurance carrier no longer accepts new BOLI business, it could have a significant impact on the future performance of the BOLI. Management will evaluate and monitor such a situation closely.
- Poor financial results of carrier. If the annual (or more frequent) carrier credit analysis shows poor financial results from the carrier, Management will evaluate this in light of the carrier's peers.
- Carrier service issues. BOLI is a long-term asset, and a carrier's commitment to servicing the BOLI is critical to its success. If the carrier is unable to continue to meet the Institution's servicing needs, Management will evaluate alternatives.
- Unavailable internal upgrades. BOLI products have evolved over the years, and will likely continue to do so. If the carrier is unable or unwilling to improve its BOLI relative to the carrier's peers, it could impact the long-term success of the BOLI program. Management will evaluate alternatives.

- Underwriting improvements. An insured employee or director can experience improvement in health or conditions that initially led to substandard mortality ratings from a carrier. If the carrier is unwilling or unable to modify such mortality ratings, Management will evaluate alternatives.
- Wholesale strategy changes. The Institution may change its strategy regarding BOLI. For example, considerations of (i) general account vs. separate account BOLI, or (ii) new money vs. portfolio crediting methods or (iii) MEC vs. non-MEC structures could change. As a result, the initial carrier or policies chosen may no longer be appropriate for the new strategy.

B.4 Reputation Risk

To avoid the risk to earnings and capital arising from negative publicity regarding the Institution's business practice, the Institution will only insure (a) members of the Board, or (b) employees who are in the top 35% (based on compensation) of full-time employee positions, and who also consent in writing to be insured, including full disclosure that the Institution intends to retain the policy even after separation from service. The amount of net life insurance purchased on any single employee will not exceed 20 times compensation.

B.5 Vendor Selection

The Board has approved the following list of BOLI vendor(s) with which the Institution may transact business:

____

The vendor selection process includes the following qualifications; and for any additional firms to be considered, Management must document the following:

- A review to determine the vendor's financial soundness and ability to honor its long-term commitments. The review may include analysis of the vendor's current audited financial statements, Section 404 audit, annual reports, credit reports, etc., and should consider a vendor's capital strength and operating results.

- An inquiry to peer institutions and state or national banking trade associations into the general reputation of the vendor for financial stability and fair and honest dealings with customers.
- An inquiry, as appropriate, into the background of the sales representatives to determine their experience and expertise.
- An inquiry into the vendor's commitment to investing in the operational infrastructure necessary to support BOLI, including, as appropriate, on-site visits.

Management must submit this information to the Board for approval prior to entering into a transaction with a previously unapproved vendor.

B.6 Retaining Policies Post-Termination

In accordance with the Interagency Statement, the Institution intends to retain ownership of the BOLI as a corporate asset even after the employer/employee relationship (or Board service) is terminated. The Institution believes that retention of BOLI provides the safest method of cost recovery for employee benefits, and that requiring written informed consent prior to implementation helps manage Reputation Risk associated with retention.

APPENDIX B

No. 010/November 14,1985
Financial Accounting Series
FASB Technical Bulletin No. 85-4

Title: Accounting for Purchases of Life Insurance

References:

- AICPA Accounting Interpretation. "Accounting for Key-Man Life Insurance"
- FASB Concepts Statement No. 3, *Elements of Financial Statements of Business Enterprises,* paragraphs 19 and 123

Question

2. How should an entity[1] account for an investment in life insurance?

---

[1] The provisions of this Technical Bulletin apply to all entities that purchase life insurance in which the entity is either the owner or beneficiary of the contract, without regard to the funding objective of the purchase. Such purchases would typically include those intended to meet loan covenants or to fund deferred-compensation agreements, buy-sell agreements, or post-employment death benefits. Purchases of life insurance by retirement plans that are subject to FASB Statement No. 35 *Accounting and Reporting by Defined Benefit Pension Plans,* are not addressed by this Technical Bulletin.

Response

2. The amount that could be realized under the insurance contract as of the date of the statement of financial position should be reported as an asset. The change in cash surrender or contract value during the period is an adjustment of premiums paid in determining the expense or income to be recognized under the contract for the period.

Effective Date and Transition

3. The provisions of this Technical Bulletin are effective for insurance policies acquired after November 14, 1985.

The Financial Accounting Standards Board has authorized its staff to prepare FASB Technical Bulletins to provide guidance on certain financial accounting and reporting problems on a timely basis, pursuant to the procedures described in FASB Technical Bulletin No. 79-1 (Revised), Purpose and Scope of FASB Technical Bulletins and Procedures for Issuance. The provisions of Technical Bulletins need not be applied to immaterial items.

BACKGROUND

4. In November 1970, the AICPA issued an Accounting Interpretation entitled, "Accounting for Key-Man Life Insurance." That Accounting Interpretation identified the cash surrender value method as generally accepted accounting for purchases of life insurance. New types of life insurance contracts, new provisions in traditional contracts, and changes in the insurance industry have led some to question the 1970 Accounting Interpretation. In October 1984, the AICPA'S Accounting Standards Executive Committee (AcSEC) approved an Issues Paper entitled, "Accounting for Key-Person Life Insurance." In the Issues Paper, AcSEC reaffirmed support of the cash surrender value method as the only generally accepted method. The AcSEC position differed from the position of the AICPA Insurance Companies Committee, which supported use of a different method in certain circumstances. AcSEC was concerned that diversity would develop in practice

because of the difference between those positions, and requested that the FASB consider the matter.

5. A premium paid by a purchaser of life insurance serves a variety of purposes. A portion of the premium pays the insurer for assumption of mortality risk and provides for recovery of the insurer's contract acquisition, initiation, and maintenance costs. Another portion of the premium contributes to the accumulation of contract values. The relative amounts of premium payments credited to various contract attributes change over time as the age of the insured party increases, and as earnings are credited to previously established contract values.
6. An insurance contract is significantly different from most investment agreements. The various attributes of the policy could be obtained separately through term insurance and purchase of investments. The combination of benefits and contract values could not, however, typically be acquired absent the insurance contract. Continued protection from mortality risk and realization of scheduled increases in contract

accumulation usually requires payments of future premiums.

7. The payment of insurance premiums may take a number of different forms. The insurance contract may be purchased through payment of a single premium, as opposed to the typical series of future premiums. Alternatively, the premium payments may be made through loans from the insurance company, which are secured by policy cash surrender values. The pattern of premium payments is a decision that does not alter the underlying nature of the insurance contract.

Consideration of Comments Received on Proposed Technical Bulletin

8. A proposed Technical Bulletin, *Accounting for Business-Owned Life Insurance,* was released for comment on June 28, 1985. Forty-seven letters of comments were received on the proposed Technical Bulletin. Certain of the comments received and consideration of them are discussed in the following paragraphs.

9. Some respondents view the dominant objective of a life insurance contract to be an investment. Subject to certain criteria evidencing an intent to continue the contract, they maintain that the contract meets the definition of an asset established in paragraph 19 of Concepts Statement 3, which states, "Assets are probable future economic benefits obtained or controlled by a particular entity as a result of past transactions or events." Those who hold this view suggested that such contracts should be accounted for using methods that result in reporting the investment in life insurance at amounts different from those stipulated in the contract.
10. This Technical Bulletin does not take that view. The current capacity to realized contract benefits is limited to settlement amounts specified in the contract. Additional amounts in excess of cash surrender value, which would be reported as assets under the various alternative accounting methods suggested, are created by future events, which typically include premium payments and earnings credited to contract amounts.

11. Paragraph 123 of Concepts Statement 3 discusses the occurrence of past events and the role of future events in the recognition of assets.

    Since the transaction or event giving rise to the enterprise's right to the future economic benefit must already have occurred, the definition excludes from assets items that may in the future become an enterprise's assets but have not yet become its assets. An enterprise has no asset for a particular future economic benefit if the transactions or events that give it access to and control of the benefit are yet in the future.

12. Some respondents asserted that reporting an insurance investment at its realizable value represents an accounting based on liquidation values. Those respondents suggested that the entity acquiring an insurance contract is, in many cases, economically or contractually committed to maintain the contract in force. They maintained that such a commitment virtually assures that benefits in excess of premiums paid would be realized and that the policy should be

reported on a basis other than its cash surrender value.

13. This Technical Bulletin does not accept that view. The amount realizable under an insurance investment represents settlement values agreed to by an independent buyer and seller. The variety of yields and contract accumulation patterns available in the insurance marketplace provides the buyer and seller a variety of insurance and settlement options. There is no compelling justification to depart from the recording of such contracts based on agreed provisions. The commitment referred to by respondents is, in the staff's view, a commitment to ensure that assets are available to meet contractual obligations. The presence of such a commitment does not change the measurement of the asset that is expected to satisfy the obligation.

14. Some respondents asserted that policy features, most notably the business exchange rider, were significant factors in determining the proper accounting for the policy. The business exchange rider allows a company to use values in an existing policy to insure a different

employee when the originally insured employee leaves the company. They maintain that this feature gives the employer the ability to transfer the contract freely and enhances the employer's ability to realize the future value of the investment. They further maintain that the increased probability of realizing future values should lead to reporting of amounts in excess of cash surrender value.

15. This Technical Bulletin rejects that view. The business exchange rider is a significant development in the design of business insurance products and reduces additional policy costs if a covered employee leaves the company. Such a provision does not affect the realization of future benefits under the insurance contract, nor does it change the traditional underwriting decisions involved in insuring a new life. Instead, the provision only reduces the cost of obtaining those benefits by allowing a new employee to be insured without the costs that are typically associated with obtaining a new policy.

APPENDIX C

VARIOUS RISK CATEGORIES AND WEIGHTS FOR BANK ASSETS

CAPITAL ADEQUACY BALANCE SHEET

The Federal Reserve, Controller of the Currency and Federal Deposit Insurance Commission have adopted risk-based capital guidelines to help evaluate and regulate banks and bank holding companies. The Office of Thrift Supervision has adopted similar guidelines for savings banks. All financial institutions are now familiar with the Tier 1, Tier 2 and leveraged ratios that must be calculated. The intent of this regulation is to create a profile which shows the risk factor in balance sheet assets and off balance sheet commitments. BOLI has a balance sheet presence and will have an impact on capital adequacy ratios. The significance of this impact depends on the assets the financial organization uses to purchase its BOLI plan. The table on page 218 outlines the various risk categories and weights for bank assets.

Off balance sheet risks are included through equivalents, again depending on the appropriate risk weight classification.

When a financial institution sells a U.S. Treasury Bond in order to generate resources to purchase a BOLI plan, it is also moving this resource from a risk weight of 0 percent to a risk weight of 100 percent. Alternative, if the bank asset sold is an agency bond or Collateralized Mortgage Obligation (CMO), the impact on capital adequacy would be less than using cash or a U.S. Treasury because of the weighting differential. An example of how BOLI will impact Capital Adequacy (in millions) is on page 219.

VARIOUS RISK CATEGORIES AND WEIGHTS FOR BANK ASSETS		
Risk Category	Definition	Risk Weighting
1	Cash and direct debt of the U.S. government and its agencies.	0%
2	Claims on domestic depository Institutions, debt unconditionally guaranteed by the U.S. government, and debt of government-sponsored agencies.	20%
3	Accruing loans secured by first liens on one-to-four family residences, mortgaged-backed securities backed by conventional mortgages and certain state or local revenue bonds or revenue-backed obligations.	50%

CAPITAL ADEQUACY BALANCE SHEET (IN MILLIONS)					
		Risk Category			
		0%	20%	50%	100%
U.S Treasuries	$2,000	$2,000			
U.S Agencies	$750		$750		
Residential Real Estate Loans	$3,000			$3,000	
Other Loans	$7,000				$7,000
Other Assets	$400				$400
Total Assets	**$13,150**				
Risk-Weighted Assets		0+	$150+	$1,500+	$7,400
Total Risk Weighted Assets..$9,050					

	Tier 1		Tier 2		
Shareholders' Equity	$950				
Capital Notes			$150		
Loan Reserve			$110		
Total	**$950**	**+**	**$260**	**=**	**$1,210**

EFFECT OF BOLI INVESTMENT ON CAPITAL RATIO (refer to page 213)		
	Tier 1 *Regulatory Minimum 4.0%*	Tier 2 *Regulatory Minimum 8.0%*
Pre-BOLI Investment Capital Ratio *	10.50%	13.37%
Post-BOLI Investment Capital Ratio		
Scenario 1: Sells U.S. Treasury bond to invest $200 million in BOLI	10.27%	13.08%
Scenario 2: Sells a CMO to invest $200 million in BOLI	10.38%	13.22%

**Capital as a percentage of risk-weighted assets.*

APPENDIX D

Sample Bank CONSOLIDATED INCOME STATEMENT $100,000.000 PURCHASE ILLUSTRATION			
	(in thousands, except per share data)		
	FY	Pro Forma	Change
Interest Income			
Interest and Fees on Loans and Leases	$735,530		
Interest on Securities			
Taxable	169,316	$163,236	(6,080)[1]
Exempt from Income Taxes	16,436		
Total Interest on Securities	185,752		
Interest on Other Short-Term Investments	1,019		
Total Interest Income	922,301	916,221	(6,080)
Interest Expense			
Interest on Deposits			
Interest Checking	25,572		
Savings	14,511		
Money Market	40,326		
Other Time	194,375		
Certificates - $100,000 and Over	13,135		
Foreign Office	24,165		
Total Interest on Deposits	312,084		
Interest on Federal Funds Borrowed	34,925		
Interest on Short-Term Bank Notes	20,285		
Interest on Long-Term Debt and Notes	12,436		
Total Interest Expense	405,548	405,548	-
Net Interest Income	516,753	510,673	(6,080)
Provision for Credit Losses	35,780	35,780	-
Net Interest Income After Provision for Credit Losses	480,973	474,893	(6,080)
Other Operating Income			
Trust Operating Income	55,238		
Service Charges on Deposit	60,905		
Data Processing Income	64,394		
Other Service Charges and Fees	74,978	80,878	5,900[2]
Securities Gains	393		
Total Other Operating Income	255,908	261,808	5,900
Operating Expenses			
Salary and Wages	144,513		
Employee Benefits	36,710		
Equipment Expenses	16,045		
Net Occupancy Expenses	26,137		
Other Operating Expenses	148,140		
Total Operating Expenses	371,545	371,545	-
Income before Income Taxes	365,336	365,156	(180)
Applicable Income Taxes	120,877	118,749	(2,128)[3]
Net Income	$244,459	$246,407	$1,948
Net Income Per Share	$3.80	$3.83	$0.03

See following page for Assumptions and Footnotes to Pro Forma

ASSUMPTIONS
• Sell $100 million in Agency mortgage-backed securities (one to five year maturity) with an estimated annual yield of 6.08%. • Buy $100 million of BOLI (PEP) with an annual yield of 5.9%. • Sample Bank's Federal tax rate is 35%.

FOOTNOTES TO PRO FORMA
[1] The interest income that the bank earned on $100 million in Agency Mortgage-banked securities at 6.08% (for example, $6.08 million) is reversed out of the amount of existing taxable securities interest income. [2] Income generated by a $100 million purchase of BOLI is $5.9 million. [3] Reduced interest income for the taxable securities also results in a reduced tax. Using a 35% tax rate, eliminating $6.08 million of taxable interest income results in a tax savings of $2.13 million.

ESTIMATED VALUE OF BANK-OWNED LIFE INSURANCE TO THE SHAREHOLDERS OF [SAMPLE BANK]			
	Without BOLI	**With BOLI**	**Change**
Stock Price	$48.00	$48.38	$0.38
Net Income	$244,449,000	$246,397,000	$1,948,000
EPS	$3.80	$3.83	$0.03
P/E Ratio	$12.63	$12.63	———
Market Value: Per Share	$48.00	$48.38	$0.38
Market Value: Aggregate	$3,087,776,842	$3,112,383,158	$24,606,316

This illustration is based on a $100 million BOLI transaction.

APPENDIX E

INTERNAL REVENUE CODE
1986 CODE-SUBTITLE A, CH. 1B PART IX

SEC.264. CERTAIN AMOUNTS PAID IN CONNECTION WITH INSURANCE CONTRACTS

[Sec. 264 (a)]

(a) GENERAL RULE.—No deduction shall be allowed for—

(1) Premiums paid on any life insurance policy covering the life of any officer or employee, or any person financially interested in any trade or business carried on by the tax payer, when the taxpayer is directly or indirectly a beneficiary under such policy.

(2) Any amount paid or accrued on indebtedness incurred or continued to purchase or carry a single premium life insurance, endowment, or annuity contract.

(3) Except as provided in subsection (c), any amount paid or accrued on indebtedness incurred or continued to purchase or carry life insurance, endowment, or

annuity contract (other than a single premium contract or a contract treated as a single premium contract) pursuant to a plan of purchase which contemplates the systematic direct or indirect borrowing of part or all of the increases in the cash value of such contract (either from the insurer or otherwise).

(4) Any interest paid or accrued on any indebtedness with respect to 1 or more life insurance policies owned by the taxpayer covering the life of any individual who—

(A) is an officer or employee of, or

(B) is financially interested in, any trade or business carried on by the taxpayer to the extent that the aggregate amount of such indebtedness with respect to policies covering such individual exceeds $50,000.

Paragraph (2) shall apply in respect of annuity contracts only as to contracts purchased after March 1, 1954.

Paragraph (3) shall apply only in respect to contracts purchased after August 6, 1963. Paragraph (4) shall apply with respect to contracts purchased after June 20, 1986.

Amendments

P.L. 99-514, § 1003 (a):

Act Sec. 1003 (a) amended Code Sec. 264 (a) by adding after paragraph (3) new paragraph (4) to read as above.

The above amendment applies to contracts purchased after June 20, 1986, in tax years ending after such date.

P.L. 99-514, § 1003 (b):

Act Sec. 1003 (b) amended Code Sec. 264 (a) by adding a new sentence at the end thereof to read as above.

The above amendment applies to contracts purchased after June 20, 1986, in tax years ending after such date.

P.L. 88-272, § 215 (a):

Amended subsection (a) to add paragraph (3) and to add at the end of subsection (a) the last sentence. The amendment applies with respect to contracts purchased after August 6, 1963.

[Sec. 264 (b)]

(b) CONTRACTS TREATED AS SINGLE PREMIUM CONTRACTS.—For purposes of subsection (a) (2), a contract shall be treated as a single premium contract—

(1) If substantially all the premiums on the contract are paid within a period of 4 years from the date on which the contract is purchased, or

(2) If amount is deposited after March 1, 1954, with the insurer for payment of a substantial number of future premiums on the contract.

[Sec. 264 (c)]

EXCEPTIONS.—Subsection (a) (3) shall not apply to any amount paid or accrued by a person during a taxable year on indebtedness incurred or continued as part of a plan referred to in subsection (a) (3)—

(1) If no part of 4 of the annual premiums due during the 7-year period (beginning with the date the first premium on the contract to which such plan relates was paid) is paid under such plan by means of indebtedness,

(2) If the total of the amounts paid or accrued by such person during such taxable year for which (without regard to this paragraph) no deduction would be allowable by reason of subsection (a) (3) does not exceed $100,

(3) If such amount was paid or accrued on indebtedness incurred because of an unforeseen substantial loss of income or unforeseen substantial increase in his financial obligations, or

(4) If such indebtedness was incurred in connection with his trade or business.

For purposes of applying paragraph (1), if there is a substantial increase in the premiums on a contract, a new 7-year period described in such paragraph with respect to such contract shall commence on the date the first such increased premium is paid.

Amendments

P.L. 88-272, § 215 (b):

Amended section 264 to add subsection (c) above. The amendment applies with respect to amounts paid or accrued in taxable years beginning after December 31, 1963.

APPENDIX F

INTERNAL REVENUE CODE 1986 CODE-SUBTITLE F, CH. 79 DEFINITIONS

[Sec. 7702]

SEC. 7702 LIFE INSURANCE CONTRACT DEFINED.

[Sec. 7702 (a)]

(a) GENERAL RULE.—For purposes of this title, the term "life insurance contract" means any contract which is a life insurance contract under the applicable law, but only if such contract—

(1) meets the cash value accumulation test of subsection (b), or

(2) (A) meets the guideline premium requirements of subsection (c), and

(3) (B) falls within the cash value corridor of subsection (d).

[Sec. 7702 (b)]

(b) CASH VALUE ACCUMULATION TEST FOR SUBSECTION (a) (1).—

(1) IN GENERAL.—A contract meets the cash value accumulation test of this subsection if, by the terms of the

contract, the cash surrender value of such contract may not at anytime exceed the net single premium which would have to be paid at such time to fund future benefits under the contract.

(2) RULES FOR APPLYING PARAGRAPH (1).—Determinations under paragraph (1) shall be made—

(A) on the basis of interest at the greater of an annual effective rate of 4 percent or the rate or rates guaranteed on issuance of the contract.

(B) on the basis of the rules of subparagraph (B) (i) (and, in the case of qualified additional benefits, subparagraph (B) (ii) of subsection (c) (3), and

(C) by taking into account under subparagraphs (A) and (D) of subsection (e) (1) only current and future death benefits and qualified additional benefits.

Amendments

P.L. 99-514, § 1825 (a) (2):

Act Sec. 1825 (a) (2) amended Code Sec. 7702 (b) (2) (C) by striking out "subparagraphs (A) and (C)" and inserting in lieu thereof "subparagraphs (A) and (D)."

The above amendment is effective as if included in the provisions of P.L. 98-369 to which such amendment relates.

[Sec, 7702 (c)]

(c) GUIDELINE PREMIUM REQUIREMENTS.—For purposes of this section—

(1) IN GENERAL.—A contract meets the guideline premium requirements of this subsection if the sum of the premiums paid under such contract does not at any time exceed the guideline premium limitation as of such time.

(2) GUIDELINE PREMIUM LIMITATION.-The term "guideline premium limitation" means, as of any date, the greater of—

(A) the guideline single premium, or

(B) the sum of the guideline level premiums to such date.

(3) GUIDELINE SINGLE PREMIUM.-

(A) IN GENERAL.-The term "guideline single premium" means the premium at issue with respect to future benefits under the contract.

(B) BASIS ON WHICH DETERMINATION IS MADE.-The determination under subparagraph (A) shall be based on-

(i) Reasonable mortality charges which meet the requirements (if any) prescribed in regulations and which (except as provided in regulations) do not exceed the mortality charges specified in the prevailing commissioner's standard tables (as defined in section 807 (d) (d)) as of the time the contract is issued,

(ii) Any reasonable charges (other than mortality charges) which (on the basis of the company's experience, if any, with respect to similar contracts) are reasonably expected to be actually paid, and

(iii) Interest at the greater of an annual effective rate of 6 percent or the rate or rates guaranteed on issuance of the contract.

(D) WHEN DETERMINATION MADE.—Except as provided in subsection (f) (7), the determination under subparagraph (A) shall be made as of the time the contract is issued.

(E) SPECIAL RULES FOR SUBPARAGRAPH (B) (ii).—

(i) CHARGES NOT SPECIFIED IN THE CONTRACT.—If any charge is not specified in the contract, the amount taken into account under subparagraph (B) (ii) for such charge shall be zero.

(ii) NEW COMPANIES, ETC.—If any company does not have adequate experience for purposes of the determination under subparagraph (B) (ii), to the extent provided in regulations, such determination shall be made on the basis of the industry-wide experience.

(4) GUIDELINE LEVEL PREMIUM.-The term "guideline level premium" means the level annual amount, payable over a period not ending before the insured attains age 95, computed on the same basis as the guideline single premium, except that paragraph (3) (B) (iii) shall be applied by substituting "4 percent" for "6 percent".

Amendments

P.L. 100-647, § 501 (a):

Act Sec. 501 (a) amended Code Sec. 7702 (c) (3) (B) by striking out clauses (i) and (ii) and inserting in lieu thereof new clauses (i) and (ii) to read as above. Prior to amendment, Code Sec. 7702 (c) (3) (B) (i)-(ii) read as follows:

(i) the mortality charges specified in the contract (or, if none is specified, the mortality charges used in determining the statutory reserves for such contract),

(ii) any changes (not taken into account under clause (i) specified in the contract (the amount of any charge not so specified shall be treated as zero), and

P.L. 100-647, § 5011 (b):

Act Sec. 5011 (b) amended Code Sec. 7702 (c) (3) by adding at the end thereof a new subparagraph (D) to read as above.

The above amendments apply to contracts entered into on or after October 21, 1988

[Sec. 7702 (d)]

(d) CASH VALUE CORRIDOR FOR PURPOSES OF SUBSECTION (a) (2) (B).—For purposes of this section—

(1) IN GENERAL.—A contract falls within the cash value corridor of this subsection if the death benefit under the contract at any time is not less than the applicable percentage of the cash surrender value.

(2) APPLICABLE PERCENTAGE.—See the following

In the case of an insured with an attained age as of the beginning of the contract year of:		*The applicable percentage shall decrease by a ratable portion for each full year:*	
More than:	But not more than:	From:	To:
0	40	250	250
40	45	250	215
45	50	215	185
50	55	185	150
55	60	150	130
60	65	130	120
65	70	120	115
70	75	115	105
75	90	105	105
90	95	105	100

page for chart.

[Sec. 7702 (e)]

(e) COMPUTATIONAL RULES.-

(1) IN GENERAL.—For purposes of this section (other than subsection (d))—

(A) the death benefit (and any qualified additional benefit) shall be deemed not to increase,

(B) the maturity date, including the date on which any benefit described in subparagraph (C) is payable, shall be deemed to be no earlier than the day on which the insured attains age 95, and no later than the day on which the insured attains age 100,

(C) the death benefits shall be deemed to be provided until the maturity date determined by taking into account subparagraph (B), and

(D) the amount of any endowment benefit (or sum of endowment benefits, including any cash surrender value on the maturity date determined by taking into account subparagraph (B)) shall be deemed not to exceed the least amount payable as a death benefit at any time under the contract.

(2) LIMITED INCREASES IN DEATH BENEFIT PERMITTED.—Notwithstanding paragraph (1) (A)—

(A) for purposes of computing the guideline level premium, an increase in the death benefit which is provided in the contract may be taken into account but only to the extent necessary to prevent a decrease in the excess of the death benefits over the cash surrender value of the contract,

(B) for the purposes of the cash value accumulation test, the increase described in subparagraph (A) may be taken into account if the contract will meet such test at all times assuming that the net level reserve (determined as if level annual premiums were paid for the contract over a period not ending before the insured attains age 95) is substituted for the net single premium,

(C) for purposes of the cash value accumulation test, the death benefit increases may be taken into account if the contract--

(i) has an initial death benefit of $5,000 or less and a maximum death benefit of $25,000 or less,

(ii) provides for a fixed predetermined annual increase not to exceed 10 percent of the initial death benefit or 8 percent of the death benefit at the end of the preceding year, and

(iii) was purchased to cover payment of burial expenses or in connection with prearranged funeral expenses.

For purposes of subparagraph (C), the initial death benefit of a contract shall be determined by treating all contracts issued to the same contract owner as 1 contract.

Amendments

P.L. 99-514 § 1825 (a) (1) (A)-(D):

Act Sec. 1825 (a) (1) (A)-(D) amended Code Sec. 7702 (e) (1) by striking out "shall be no earlier than" in subparagraph (B) and inserting in lieu thereof "shall be deemed to be no earlier than", by striking out "and" at the end of subparagraph (B), by redesignating subparagraph (C) as subparagraph (D) and inserting after subparagraph (B) new subparagraph (C) to read as above, and striking out "the maturity date described in subparagraph (B)" in subparagraph (D) (as so redesignated) and inserting in lieu thereof "the maturity date determined by taking into account subparagraph (B)".

The above amendment is effective as if included in the provisions of P.L. 98-369 to which such amendments relates.

P.L. 99-514, § 1825 (A) (3):

Act Sec. 1825 (a) (3) amended Code Sec. 7702 (e) (1) by inserting "(other than subsection (d))" after "section."

The above amendment is effective as if included in the provisions of P.L. 98-369 to which such amendment relates.

P.L. 99-154, § 1825 (a) (4) (A)-(C):

Act Sec. 1825 (a) (4) (A)-(C) amended Code Sec. 7702 (e) (2) by striking out "and" at the end of subparagraph (A), by striking out the period at the end of subparagraph (B), and inserting in lieu thereof a comma and "and", and by adding at the end thereof new subparagraph (C) to read as above.

The above amendment is effective with respect to contracts entered into after October 22, 1986 [effective date changed by P.L. 100-647, § 1018 (j)].

[Sec. 7702 (f)]

(f) OTHER DEFINITIONS AND SPECIAL RULES.—For purposes of this section—

(1) PREMIUMS PAID—

A) IN GENERAL.—The term "premiums paid" means the premiums paid under the contract less amounts (other than amounts includible in gross income) to which section 72 (e) applies and less any excess premiums with respect to which there is a distribution described in subparagraph (B) or (E) of paragraph (7) and any other amounts received with respect to the contract which are specified in regulations.

(B) TREATMENT OF CERTAIN PREMIUMS RETURNED TO POLICYHOLDER.—If, in order to comply with the requirements of subsection (a) (2) (A), any portion of any premium paid any contract year is returned by the insurance company (with interest) within 60 days after the end of a contract year, the amount so returned (excluding interest) shall be deemed to reduce the sum of the premiums paid under the contract during such year.

(C) INTEREST RETURNED INCLUDIBLE IN GROSS INCOME.—Notwithstanding the provisions of section 72 (e), the amount of any interest returned as provided in subparagraph (B) shall be includible in the gross income of the recipient.

(2) CASH VALUES—

(A) CASH SURRENDER VALUE.-The cash surrender value of any contract shall be its cash value determined without regard to any surrender charge, policy, loan, or reasonable termination dividends.

(B) NET SURRENDER VALUE.-The net surrender value of any contract shall be determined with regard to surrender charges but without regard to any policy loan.

(3) DEATH BENEFIT.-The term "death benefit" means the amount payable by reason of the death of the

insured (determined without regard to any qualified additional benefits).

(4) FUTURE BENEFITS.-The term "future benefits" means death benefits and endowment benefits.

(5) QUALIFIED ADDITIONAL BENEFITS.—

(A) IN GENERAL.—The term "qualified additional benefits" means any —

(i) guaranteed insurability,

(ii) accidental death or disability benefit,

(iii) family term coverage,

(iv) disability waiver benefit, or

(v) other benefit prescribed under regulations

(B) TREATMENT OF QUALIFIED ADDITIONAL BENEFITS.—For purposes of this section, qualified additional benefits shall not be treated as future benefits under the contract, but the charges for such benefits shall be treated as future benefits.

(C)TREATMENT OF OTHER ADDITIONAL BENEFITS.—In the case of any additional benefit which is not a qualified additional benefit—

(i) such benefit shall be treated as a future benefit, and

(ii) any charge for such benefit which is not prefunded shall be treated as a premium.

(6) PREMIUM PAYMENTS NOT DISQUALIFYING CONTRACT.-The payment of a premium which would result in the sum of the premiums paid exceeding the guideline premium limitation shall be disregarded for purposes of subsection (a) (2) if the amount of such premium does not exceed the amount necessary to prevent the termination of the contract on or before the end of the contract year (but only if the contract will have no cash surrender value at the end of such extension period).

(7) ADJUSTMENTS.-

(A) IN GENERAL.-If there is a change in the benefits under (or in other terms of) the contract which was not reflected in any previous determination or adjustment made under this section, there shall be proper adjustments in future determinations made under this section.

(B) RULE OF CERTAIN CHANGES DURING FIRST 15 YEARS.—If—

(i) a change described in subparagraph (A) reduces benefits under the contract,

(ii) the change occurs during the 15-year period beginning on the issue date of the contract, and

(iii) a cash distribution is made to the policyholder as a result of such change,

section 72 (other than subsection (e) (5(thereof) shall apply to such cash distribution to the extent it does not exceed the recapture ceiling determined under subparagraph (C) or (D) (whichever applies).

(C) RECAPTURE CEILING WHERE CHANGE OCCURS DURING THE FIRST 5 YEARS.—If the change referred to in subparagraph (B) (ii) occurs during the 5-year period beginning on the issue date of the contract, the recapture ceiling is—

(i) in the case of a contract to which subsection (a) (1) applies, the excess of-

(I) the cash surrender value of the contract, immediately before the reduction, over

(II) the net single premium (determined under subsection (b)), immediately after the reduction, or

(ii) in the case of a contract to which subsection (a) (2) applies, the greater of—

(I) the excess of the aggregate premiums paid under the contract, immediately before the reduction, over the guideline premium limitation for the contract (determined under subsection (c) (2), taking into account the adjustment described in subparagraph (A)), or

(II) the excess of the cash surrender value of the contract, immediately before the reduction, over the cash value corridor of subsection (d) (determined immediately after the reduction).

(D) RECAPTURE CEILING WHERE CHANGE OCCURS AFTER 5TH YEAR AND BEFORE 16TH.-If the change referred to in subparagraph (B) occurs after the 5-year period referred to under subparagraph (C), the recapture ceiling is the excess of the cash surrender value of the contract, immediately before the reduction, over the cash value corridor of subsection (d) (determined immediately after the reduction and whether or not subsection (d) applies to the contract).

(E) TREATMENT OF CERTAIN DISTRIBUTIONS MADE IN ANTICIPATION OF BENEFIT REDUCTIONS.—Under regulations prescribed by the Secretary, subparagraph (B) shall apply also to any distribution made in anticipation of a reduction in benefits under the contract. For purposes of the preceding sentence, appropriate adjustments shall be made in the provisions of subparagraphs (C) and (D); and any distribution which reduces the cash surrender value of a contract and which is made within 2 years before a reduction in benefits under the contract shall be treated as made in anticipation of such reduction.

(8) CORRECTION OF ERRORS.—If the taxpayer establishes to the satisfaction of the Secretary that—

(A) the requirements described in subsection (a) for any contract year were not satisfied due to reasonable error, and

(B) reasonable steps are being taken to remedy the error, the Secretary may waive the failure to satisfy such requirements.

(9) SPECIAL RULE FOR VARIABLE LIFE INSURANCE CONTRACTS.—In the case of any contract which is a variable contract (as defined in section 817), the determination of whether such contract meets the requirements of subsection (a) shall be made whenever the death benefits under such contract change but not less frequently than once during each 12-month period.

Amendments

P.O. 99-514 § 1825 (b) (1):

Act Sec. 1825 (b) (1) amended Code Sec. 7702 (f) (7) to read as above. Prior to amendment, Code Sec. 7702 (f)(7) read as follows:

(7) ADJUSTMENTS—

(A) IN GENERAL.-In the event of a change in the future benefits of any qualified additional benefit (or in any other terms) under the contract which was not reflected in any previous determination made under this section, under regulations prescribed by the Secretary, there shall be proper adjustments in future determinations made under this section.

(B) CERTAIN CHANGES TREATED AS EXCHANGE.-In the case of any change which reduces the future benefits under the contract, such change shall be treated as an exchange of the contract for another contract.

The above amendment is effective as if included in the provisions of P.L. 98-369 to which such amendment relates.

P.L. 99-514, § 1805 (b) (2):

Act. Sec. 1825 (b) (2) amended Code Sec. 7702 (f)(1) (A) by striking out "less any other amounts received" and inserting in lieu thereof "less any excess premiums with respect to which there is a distribution described in subparagraph (B) or (E) of paragraph (7) and any other amounts received."

The above amendment is effective as if included in the provisions of P.L. 98-369 to which such amendment relates.

[Sec. 7702 (g)]

(g) TREATMENT OF CONTRACTS WHICH DO NOT MEET SUBSECTION (A) TEST.—

(1) INCOME INCLUSION.—

(A) IN GENERAL.-If at any time any contract which is a life insurance contract under the applicable law does not meet the definition of life insurance contract under subsection (a), the income on the contract for any taxable year of the policyholder shall be treated as ordinary income received or accrued by the policyholder during such year.

(B) INCOME ON THE CONTRACT.-For purposes of this paragraph, the term "income on the contract" means, with respect to any taxable year of the policyholder, the excess of—

(i) the sum of-

(I) the increase in the net surrender value of the contract during the taxable year, and

(II) the cost of life insurance protection provided under the contract during the taxable year, over

(ii) the premiums paid (as defined in subsection (f) (1) under the contract during the taxable year).

(C) CONTRACTS WHICH CEASE TO MEET DEFINITION.—If, during any taxable year of the policyholder, a contract which is a life insurance contract under the applicable law ceases to meet the definition of life insurance contract under subsection (a), the income on the contract for all prior taxable years shall be treated as received or accrued during the taxable year in which such cessation occurs.

(D) COST OF LIFE INSURANCE PROTECTION.—For purposes of this paragraph, the cost of life insurance protection provided under the contract shall be the lesser of—

(i) the cost of individual insurance on the life of the insured as determined on the basis of uniform premiums (computed on the basis of 5-year age brackets) prescribed by the Secretary by regulations, or

(ii) the mortality charge (if any) stated in the contract.

(2) TREATMENT OF AMOUNT PAID ON DEATH OF INSURED.-If any contract which is a life insurance contract under the applicable law does not meet the definition of life insurance contract under subsection (a), the excess of the amount paid by the reason of the death of the insured over the net surrender value of the contract should be deemed to be paid under a life insurance contract for purposes of section 101 and subtitle B.

(3) CONTRACT CONTINUES TO BE TREATED AS INSURANCE CONTRACT.-If any contract which is a life insurance contract under the applicable law does not meet the definition of life insurance contract

under subsection (a), such contract shall, notwithstanding such failure, be treated as an insurance contract for purposes of this title.

Amendments

P.L. 99.154, § 1825 (c):

Act Sec. 1825 (c) amended Code Sec. 7702 (g) (1) (B) (ii) to read as above. Prior to amendment, Code Sec. 7702 (1) (B) (ii) read as follows:

(ii) the amount of premiums paid under the contract during the taxable year reduced by policyholder dividends during such taxable year.

The above amendment is effective as if included in the provisions of P.L. 98-369 to which such amendment relates.

[Sec. 7702 (h)]

(h) ENDOWMENT CONTRACTS RECEIVE SAME TREATMENT.-

(1) IN GENERAL.-References in subsections (a) and (g) to a life insurance contract shall be treated as including references to a contract which is an endowment contract under the applicable law.

(2) DEFINITION OF ENDOWMENT CONTRACT.-For purposes of this title (other than paragraph (1)), the term "endowment contract" means as contract which is an endowment contract under the applicable law in which meets the requirements of subsection (a).

[Sec. 7702 (i)]

(i) TRANSITIONAL RULE FOR CERTAIN 20-PAY CONTRACTS.—

(1) IN GENERAL.-In the case of a qualified 20-pay contract, this section shall be applied by substituting "3 percent" for "4 percent" in subsection (b) (2)

(2) QUALIFIED 20-PAY CONTRACT.-For purposes of paragraph (1), the term "qualified 20-pay contract" means any contract which-

(A) requires at least 20 nondecreasing annual premium payments, and

(B) is issued pursuant to an existing plan of insurance.

(3) EXISTING PLAN OF INSURANCE.-For purposes of this subsection, the term "existing plan of insurance" means, with respect to any contract, any plan of insurance which was filed by the company issuing such contract in 1 or more States before September 28, 1983, and is on file in the appropriate State for such contract.

[Sec. 7702 (j)]

(j) CERTAIN CHURCH SELF FUNDED DEATH BENEFIT PLANS TREATED AS LIFE INSURANCE.—

(1) IN GENERAL.-In determining whether any plan or arrangement described in paragraph (2) is a life insurance contract, the requirement of subsection (a) that the contract be a life insurance contract under applicable law shall not apply.

(2) DESCRIPTION—For purposes of this subsection, a plan or arrangement is described in this paragraph if—

(A) such plan or arrangement provides for the payment of benefits by reason of the death of the individuals covered under such plan or arrangement, and

(B) such plan or arrangements is provided by a church for the benefit of its employees and their beneficiaries, directly or through an organization described in section 414 (e) (3) (A) or an organization described in section 414 (e) (3) (B) (ii).

(3) DEFINITIONS.—For purposes of this subsection—

(A) CHURCH.-The term "church" means a church or a convention or association of churches.

(B) EMPLOYEE.-The term "employee" includes an employee described in section (414) (e) (3) (B)

Amendments

P.L. 100-647, § 6078 (a):

Act Sec. 6078 (a) amended Code Sec. 7702 by inserting after subsection (i) new subsection (j) to read as above.

The above amendment is effective as if included in the amendments made by section 221 (a) of the Tax Reform Act of 1984 (P.L. 98-369).

[Sec. 7702 (k)]

(k) REGULATIONS.-The Secretary shall prescribe such regulations as may be necessary or appropriate to carry out the purposes of this section.

Amendments

P.L. 100-647, § 6078 (a):

Act Sec. 6078 (a) amended Code Sec. 7702 by redesignating subsection (j) as subsection (k).

The above amendment is effective as if included in the amendments made by section 221 (a) of the Tax Reform Act of 1984 (P.L. 98-369) to which it relates.

P.L. 98-369, § 221 (a):

Act Sec. 221 (a) added Code Sec. 7702, above.

The above amendment applies to contracts issued after December 31, 1984, in tax years ending after such date. Special rules appear below.

P.L. 98-369, § 221 (d) (2)-(5), as amended by P.L. 99-514, § 1825 (e):

(2) Special rule for certain contracts issued after June 30, 1984.–

(A) General Rule.-Except as otherwise provided in this paragraph, the amendments made by this section shall apply also to any contract issued after June 30, 1984, which provides an increasing death benefit and has premium funding more rapid than 10-year level premium payments.

(B) Exception for certain contracts.—Subparagraph (A) shall not apply to any contract if-

(i) such contract (whether or not a flexible premium contract) would meet the requirements of section 101 (f) of the Internal Revenue Code of 1954,

(ii) such contract is not a flexible premium life insurance contract (within the meaning of section 101 (f) of such Code) and would meet the requirements of section 7702 of such Code determined by-

(I) substituting "3 percent" for "4 percent" in section 7702 (b) (2) of such Code, and

(II) treating subparagraph (B) of section 7702 (e) (1) of such Code as if it reads as follows: "the maturity date shall be the latest maturity date permitted under the contract, but no less than 20 years after the date of issue or (if earlier) age 95", or

(iii) under such contract-

(I) the premiums (including any policy fees) will be adjusted from time-to-time to reflect the level amount necessary (but not less than zero) at the time of such adjustment to provide a level death benefit assuming interest crediting and an annual effective interest rate of not less than 3 percent, or

(II) at the option of the insured, in lieu of an adjustment under subclause (I) there will be a comparable adjustment in the amount of the death benefit.

(C) Certain contracts issued before October 1, 1984.-

(i) In general.-Subparagraph (A) shall be applied by substituting "September 30, 1984" for "June 30, 1984" thereof in this case of a contract-

(I) which would meet the requirements of section 7702 of such Code if "3 percent" were substituted for "4 percent" in section 7702 (b) (2) of such Code, and the rate or rates guaranteed on issuance of the contract were determined without regard to any mortality charges and any initial excess interest guarantees, and

(II) the cash surrender value of which does not at any time exceed the net single premium which would have to be paid at such time to fund future benefits under the contract.

(ii) Definitions.—For purposes of clause (j)-

(I) In general.-Except as provided in subclause (II), terms used in clause (i) shall have the same meanings as when used in section 7702 of such Code.

(II) Net single premium.-The term "net single premium" shall be determined by substituting "3 percent" for "4 percent" in section 7702 (b) (2) of such Code, by using 1958 standard ordinary mortality and morbidity tables of the National Association of Insurance Commissioners, and by assuming a level of death benefit.

(3) Transitional rule for certain existing plans of insurance.-A plan of insurance on file in 1 or more States before September 28, 1983, shall be treated for purposes of section 7702 (i) (3) of such Code as a plan of insurance on file in 1 or more States before September 28, 1983, without regard to whether such plan of insurance is modified after September 28, 1983, to permit the crediting of excess interest or similar amounts annually and not monthly under contracts issued pursuant to such plan of insurance.

(4) Extension of flexible premium contract provisions.-The amendments made by subsection (b) shall take effect on January 1, 1984.

(5) Special rule of master contract.-For purposes of this subsection, in the case of a master contract, the date taken into account with respect to any insured shall

be the first date on which such insured is covered under such contract.

[Sec. 7702 A]

Sec. 7702 A. MODIFIED ENDOWMENT CONTRACT DEFINED.

[Sec. 7702 A (a)]

(a) GENERAL RULE.—For purposes of section 72, the term "modified endowment contract" means any contract meeting the requirements of section 7702—

(1) which—

(A) is entered into on or after June 21, 1988, and

(B) fails to meet the 7-pay test of subsection (b), or

(2) which is received in exchange for a contract described in paragraph (1)

[Sec. 7702 A (b)]

(b) 7-PAY TEST.—For purposes of subsection (a), a contract fails to meet the 7-pay test of this subsection if the accumulated amount paid under the contract at any time during the 1st 7 contract years exceeds the sum of the net level premiums which would have been paid on or before such time if the contract provided for paid-up future benefits after the payments of 7 level annual premiums.

[Sec. 7702 A (c)]

(c) COMPUTATIONAL RULES.—

(1) IN GENERAL.– Except as provided in this subsection, the determination under subsection (b) of the 7 level annual premiums shall be made—

(A) as of the time the contract is issued, and by applying the rules of section 7702 (b) (2) and of section 7702 (e) (other than paragraph (2) (C) thereof), except that the death benefit provided for the 1st contract year shall be deemed to be provided until the maturity date without regard to any scheduled reduction after the 1st 7 contract years.

(2) REDUCTION IN BENEFITS DURING FIRST 7 YEARS.

APPENDIX G

TYPICAL TIMELINE FOR BOLI IMPLEMENTATION (FROM DATE OF DECISION)										
	Wk 1	Wk 2	Wk 3	Wk 4	Wk 5	Wk 6	Wk 7	Wk 8	Wk 9	Wk 10
Product/Carrier Selection	■									
Finalize Census to Be Insured	■									
Execute Binder and Master Application		■								
Insurable Interest Determination		■	■							
BC 249 Calculation		■	■							
Design Employee Communications		■	■							
Employee Notification/ Enrollment				■	■	■	■	■		
Reconcile Employee Census to Carrier						■	■	■	■	
Final Premium Billing/ Reconciliation								■	■	
Present Master Contract/List of Insureds										■
Administration Meeting										■

APPENDIX H

[SAMPLE BANK]

EMPLOYEE LETTER REQUESTING CONSENT

June 1, 2006

Dear Employee:

[Sample Bank] is implementing a new Bank-Owned Life Insurance Program. This program allows the corporation to attractively finance its employee benefit plan liabilities.

Under the plan, [Sample Bank] will purchase life insurance on a group of employees. [Sample Bank] will be the owner and the beneficiary of these policies.

There is no cost to you to participate, nor will your participation have any effect on your company-provided or personal life insurance programs, or other benefit plans.

This type of plan has been implemented by many of America's largest financial institutions as a means of helping to meet employee benefit plan liabilities. We believe it is appropriate for [Sample Bank] and its employees, and we fully support your participation.

Please return the attached form by [enrollment date], indicating your decision.

Please complete your card today and send it back to your Human Resources Department. If you have any questions, please call our consultant at 1-800-555-5555.

Sincerely,

[SAMPLE BANK]

BANK OWNED LIFE INSURANCE INFORMATION PAMPHLET

A Substantial Benefit for [Our Bank] and its Employees

[Our Bank] is pleased to announce a new Bank-Owned Life Insurance Plan. This plan has benefits for both [Our Bank] and our employees. Bank-Owned Life Insurance (BOLI) is an investment for the company that relies on the support and participation of our employees. This program will provide:

- [Our Bank] with an additional, cost-effective source of funds that will help finance [Our Bank's] business needs, including our employee benefits programs.
- [Our Bank] with a cash benefit upon your death, although under the BOLI program, the longer you live, the greater the financial benefit to [Our Bank].

This partnering with our employees provides another way for [Our Bank] to reduce costs and improve profitability. And as a result, you may receive an additional indirect benefit because as [Our Bank's] profitability improves, the annual percentage of your salary that the company contributes to your Retirement Savings and Profit-Sharing Plan account also increases.

Thank you in advance for your participation in this very important program.

Sincerely,

How do I participate?

To participate in the plan, please return the enclosed enrollment form

to________________________, by [enrollment date].

How will participation affect my taxes?

There is no effect on your personal taxes.

Will I need to have a health examination?

No. All you need to do is fill out the form.

Will this program affect my group term life insurance coverage provided through [Our Bank] or any other personal life insurance?

No, this coverage does not have an impact on any other life insurance or company-provided benefits you may have.

Is my participation important?

Yes. [Our Bank's] objective is 100 percent participation because the greater the participation, the greater the financial benefit to the company in its efforts to reduce costs and improve profitability.

What happens if I don't participate?

[Our Bank] will not purchase a life insurance contract on your life.

Who will record my participation?

The Plan Administrator will maintain a record of your participation.

How does the insurance program work?

[Our Bank] will purchase a life insurance policy on you. The amount of insurance is directly related to [Our Bank's] employee benefit plan expenses. [Our Bank] will pay the premium. We will be the owner of the policy, and the beneficiary of the policy records.

Is this program unique to [Our Bank]?

No, several large banks have introduced similar programs over the past few years.

What will [Our Bank] do with the money it receives from the Insurance company?

All proceeds become part of company assets and will be used for corporate financing, including employee benefit programs.

Through which company is the insurance being purchased?

[Insurance carrier], one of the financially strongest insurance companies in North America.

Can the bank cancel the program at any time?

Yes.

Whom do I call for more information?

Call a member of the Benefit Coordination Team at 1-800-555-5555 or your local human resources representative.

APPENDIX I

Consent to Insurance

____

Bank Name

____

Name of Employee/ Director of the Bank	SSN	Date of Birth	Gender

____

Resident Address (City, ST Zip)	Business Address (City, ST Zip)

I acknowledge, understand and agree that if I consent to be insured:

- A life insurance policy will be issued on my life by an Insurer selected by the Bank, and that such policy will be issued to the Bank;
- The Bank will apply for, own and control the insurance policy in every respect;
- The Bank will continue to be the owner and beneficiary of the life insurance policy indefinitely, including after my employment/service terminates for any reason; and
- The maximum aggregate face amount of the policy issued will not exceed __________________ at the time the policy is issued.

CONSENT TO INSURANCE: (Please complete)

☐ **YES** I, the undersigned, have read and understand this Consent to Insurance form, agree that the information contained herein is accurate and complete to the best of my knowledge and belief, and willingly choose to consent as indicated above. I also agree that the Insurer may rely upon the statements and answers in this form in determining the pricing and the issuance of any policy issued on my life, and that the form may be attached to and made part of the insurance policy.

☐ **NO** I do not consent to have insurance purchased on my life.

EMPLOYEE/DIRECTOR OF THE BANK

____

Signature *Date*

[*Note: The insurance carrier may have additional questions regarding the insured's "at-work" status and tobacco/nicotine usage.*]

GLOSSARY

Accredited Investor: as defined in Rule 502 of Regulation D, is any institution or individual meeting minimum net worth requirements of the purchase of securities qualifying under the Regulation D registration exemption. An accredited investor is generally accepted to be one who:

- has a net worth of $1 million or more; or
- has had an annual income of $200,000 or more in each of the most recent years (or $300,000 jointly with a spouse) and who has a reasonable expectation of reaching the same income level in the current year.

Accumulation Account: is another term for cash value, such as found within a whole life policy. However, the accumulation account of a Universal Life policy can have a negative balance, unlike the cash value account.

ACE (Adjusted Current Earnings): is an adjustment intended to reflect a corporation's pre-tax net book income as measured for financial accounting purposes. Its purpose is to ensure that a corporation which reports a profit to the public or its shareholders reports that profit to the IRS as well. To calculate ACE, the corporation begins with AMTI, adds earnings and profits (such as income on a life insurance policy and receipt of key-person insurance death proceeds), then subtracts certain deductible earnings (such as certain dividend income deductions). IRC Sec. 56 (g). The Corporation then recalculates depreciation once again according to specified methods to arrive at the final ACE adjustment. IRC Sec. 56 (g)(4)(A).

AMT (Alternative Minimum Tax): for tax years beginning in 1990 and thereafter, corporations must calculate an Adjusted Current Earnings (ACE) amount and an Alternative Minimum Taxable Income (AMTI) amount. If the ACE exceeds the AMTI amount, then 75% of the ACE amount is added to the AMTI amount. Conversely, if the AMTI exceeds ACE, a reduction in the AMTI of 75% of the difference is permitted, but this reduction cannot exceed the aggregate amount by which AMTI has been increased in prior tax years as a result of the ACE preference less the aggregate reductions allowed as a result of the preference for prior years.

AMTI (Alternative Minimum Taxable Income): IRC Sec. 55 (b)(2) is regular taxable income determined with some adjustments and increases by certain tax preferences such as accelerated depreciation versus straight line, percentage of completion method over long-term contracts, no installment sale treatment of inventory, certified pollution-control facilities depreciated under an alternative depreciation system, and mining exploration and development costs amortized over ten years (IRC Sec. 55 (a)).

Basis Point (bp): 1 basis point is equal to 1/100 of 1 percent of yield. There are 100 basis points in 1 percentage point. For example, a yield that changes from 5.50 to 5.75 has moved up by 25 basis points.

Beneficiary: designation by the owner of a life insurance policy indicating to whom the proceeds are to be paid upon the insured's death or when an endowment matures. Anyone can be named a beneficiary (relative, nonrelative, pet, charity, corporation, trustee, partnership).

Benefit Liabilities: the present and future costs incurred by a corporation associated with its employee benefit plans.

Binder Agreement: one of several closing documents, a binder is executed by the insurance carrier and a corporate purchaser in order to outline the terms for accepting a premium deposit prior to policy issue. In general, it establishes the policy date and coverage amounts prior to policy issue, has a fixed duration, and allows a provision for a deposit refund.

BOLI (Bank-Owned Life Insurance): The bank purchases life insurance on its employees in order to finance employee benefit costs and to earn a tax-free yield on its investment. The amount of purchase is based upon the expected total costs of the benefit plans during and after each employee's working lifetime for that bank. The amount of the BOLI purchased is such that it produces sufficient present value gains to equal (but which may not exceed) the present value cost of the total liabilities. The end result is that BOLI creates an immediate increase in net income and earnings per share.

Capital Adequacy Ratios: help define the structure of a bank's balance sheet in terms of risk-based capital values. These ratios give a picture of how the bank's assets are allocated among different investments. See Appendix C.

Carrier Risk: the risk associated with a change (drop) in an insurance carrier's credit rating.

Cash Value (Cash Surrender Value): money the policyowner is entitled to receive from the insurance company upon surrendering a life insurance policy with cash value. The sum is the cash value stated in the policy minus a surrender charge and any outstanding loans and interest thereon.

Cash Value Corridor Test: one of two tests applied to life insurance contracts under IRC Section 7702. A contract falls within this test if the death benefit payable under the contract at any time is at least equal to an applicable percentage of the cash surrender value. The test is in table form; see Appendix F.

Ceiling Rate (Cap): is a predetermined maximum yield on the investment. In particular, it is the top side of the buyer's potential return of the PEP life insurance product.

Census: is a demographic snapshot of eligible employees to be used in calculating who will be insured and who will not be insured. Such characteristics of the census include the total number of employees of the corporation, the average age of the employee group, sex, and the number of officers or other eligible group. Also included in the census is benefit cost information such as postretirement medical, life insurance, deferred compensation plans, and qualified retirement plans 401 (k) matching contributions, defined benefit plans etc. The census is also used to determine the amount of insurable interest the corporation has on those employees.

Chassis: refers to the basic skeletal structure of an insurance product. Examples might be interest-sensitive policies, universal policies, or variable policies.

COLI (Corporate Owned Life Insurance): insurance purchases by a corporation on the life of the employee, paid for by a corporation on the life of the employee, paid for by the company, with the company as the beneficiary. This insurance vehicle has been used to fund post-retirement employee plans, in which the cash values are listed as assets on the company's balance sheet.

Commissioners Standard Ordinary Mortality Table (CSO): table used in calculating minimum non-forfeiture value and policy reserves for ordinary life insurance policies.

These tables, which give minimum values that must be guaranteed to policyowners as approved by the National Association of Insurance Commissioners (NAIC), depict the number of people dying each year out of the original population, not as individuals, but in age groups. The 1980 CSO Table is based on the mortality of Americans evaluated with a physical examination process in 1980.

Consent: compliance or approval of what is to be done or proposed by another in the case of bank-owned life insurance.

Crediting Rate: is the yield credited to the policyowner based upon cash buildup in the policy.

Death Benefit: amount payable, as stated in a life insurance policy, upon the death of the insured. This is the face value of the policy plus any riders, less any outstanding loans and the interest accrued thereon.

Disintermediation Risk: flow of funds out of one financial instrument, whose interest rates are low, into another financial instrument, whose interest rates are higher. In the early 1980s, insurance companies experienced disintermediation as whole life polices were surrendered for their cash values and these sums were then transferred to higher interest-paying noninsurance products. Because of this situation, interest-sensitive policies were developed by insurance companies.

Dividend: sum returned to a policyowner by an insurance company under a participation policy. Dividends are not deemed as taxable distributions, as the Internal Revenue Service interprets them as a refund of a portion of the premium paid. There are several ways in which the policyowner may use dividends.

Employee Benefit Plans: provision by an employer for the economic and social welfare of employees. Generally include: (1) pension plans for retirements; (2) group life insurance for death; (3) group health insurance for illness and accident; (4) group disability income insurance for the loss of income due to illness and accident; and (5) accidental death and dismemberment. Dental insurance, eyeglass insurance, and legal expense insurance may be included. These plans are established for the reasons of morale, to reduce turnover, and for tax benefits (contributions are usually deductible as business expenses to employers and not currently taxable income to employees).

Enrollment Timeline: A schedule of steps necessary to implement a COLI/BOLI life insurance program. Upon a position decision to purchase, it begins with product/ carrier selection and moves through various steps to the closing that consists of premium payment collection and a final administration meeting. The timelines for COLI and BOLI will consist of the same steps, yet they may vary in overall length due to the nature of the products.

ERISA (Employee Retirement Income Security Act of 1974): Law that established rules and regulations to govern private pension plans, including vesting requirements, funding mechanisms, and general plan design and descriptions.

Excess Interest: amount credited by carrier to policy values over and above guaranteed interest. Derived from carrier's investment profits.

FAS 106 (Statements of Standards): Requires a corporation to accrue for the cost of postretirement benefits other than pensions.

FAS 109 (Statements of Standards): underlies the accounting for income taxes and notes that if the difference of cash surrender value over premiums paid is not temporary (as when the policy is to be held until death of the insured), policy income is free of tax.

FASB 85-4 (Technical Bulletin): is the primary accounting guide for recording the cash surrender value method of a life insurance policy. It explains how under this method, the premium payments are expensed and cash surrender values increases are reported as income.

FDIC (Federal Deposit Insurance Corporation): independent federal agency, established in 1933, that insures deposits up to $100,000 in member banks. It has its own reserves and can borrow from the U.S. Treasury, and sometimes acts to prevent bank failures, for instance, by facilitating bank mergers.

Federal Reserve Board: a seven-member group appointed by the president (subject to approval by Congress) to oversee operations of the Federal Reserve System.

Federal Reserve System (Fed): system established by the Federal Reserve Act of 1931 to regulate the U.S. monetary and banking system. The Federal Reserve System is comprised of 12 regional Federal Reserve Banks, their 25 branches, and all national and state banks that are part of the system. National banks are stockholders of the Federal Reserve Bank in their region. The Federal Reserve System's main functions are to regulate the national money supply, set reserve requirements for member banks, supervise the printing of currency at the mint, act as clearinghouse for the transfer of funds throughout the banking system, and examine member banks to make sure they meet various Federal Reserve System regulations.

Floor Rate: a predetermined, guaranteed minimum yield on an investment. In particular, it is the bottom side of the buyer's potential return of the PEP life insurance product.

Front-End Load: a sales charge paid with the first premium that is in addition to the pure cost of insurance. It reflects agent commissions, premium taxes and administrative costs associated with putting business on an insurance company's books, and contingencies.

GAAP (Generally Accepted Accounting Principles): type of accounting method, in life insurance, designed to match revenues and expenses of an insurer according to principles designed by the Financial Accounting Standards Board (FASB) and the Audit Guide for Stock Life Insurance Companies published by the American Institute of CPAs. For example, under GAAP, acquisition expenses (cost of placing insurance on a company's books such as administrative expenses and agent commissions) are recognized in the same proportion that premium income is recognized over the premium paying period, with losses subtracted from premium and investment income as they occur.

General Account Products: are life insurance products that are structured with carrier investments that are found or held within the carrier's general account (as opposed to a separate account). They are fixed-rate products with yields that reset annually based upon the investments within the general account. Because this account is the main portfolio account of the carrier, it is what helps determine the carrier's credit rating.

Guaranteed Issue: the right to purchase insurance without physical examination; the present and past physical condition of the applicant is not considered. Normally, the insurance carrier will issue coverage on all employees designated who have been actively at work for the past 90 days without interruption. The insurance carrier uses mortality tables to price the impact of issuing the coverage based on the law of large numbers.

Guideline Single Premium Test: is the premium necessary to fund future benefits under the contract, determined at time the contract is issued. This test is one of two tests used to define a life insurance contract and can be found in IRC 7702.

Insurable Interest: expectation of a monetary loss that can be covered by insurance.

Insurance: mechanism for contractually shifting burdens of a number of pure risks by pooling them.

Investment: **a** vehicle for funds, expected to maintain or increase its value and/or generate positive returns.

Investment Company Act of 1940: act that regulates the variable dollar insurance products (equity related) sold by insurance companies. The act includes regulations that stipulate: (1) the variable dollar insurance products must be funded through a separate account (segregated from the other investment accounts of the insurance company); (2) benefits and cash values must vary in tandem with the investment returns of this separate account; (3) mortality and expense fluctuations (above the maximum chargeable stipulated in the policy) must be borne by the insurance company; (4) maximum sales load; and (5) periodic financial reports must be sent to the policyowner.

Investment Grade Bonds: or "Bank Grade Bonds" are bonds that have a high credit rating and a high probability to repay their debt obligation upon maturity. For example, Standard & Poor's investment grade bonds are rated BBB or higher. Bonds below this rating are considered non-investment grade or "Speculative" bonds.

IRC Section 1035(a): also called a "1035 Exchange," allows a policyholder a tax-free exchange of a life insurance policy for another policy. The exchange may be within the existing company or to an outside company. For example, if the credit rating of a carrier drops, the policyholder may switch the policy over to a more stable carrier. They may also exchange the policy from a fixed contract to a variable contract. In any case, the exchange of the policy must be on the life of the same insured.

IRC Section 264(c): defines the owner's right of tax deductibility of interest paid due to indebtedness taken on the purchase of a single and non-single premium life insurance policies.

IRC Section 7702: is the definition of a life insurance contract. It defines the effects of taxation upon such issues as policy distributions, annuities, cash value increases, death proceeds, and policy loans. In order for a contract to be classified as a life insurance contract, it must meet one of two alternative tests; (1) the cash value accumulation test, (2) the guideline premium and cash value corridor test. See Appendix F.

IRS (Internal Revenue Service): agency of the federal government that is responsible for the administration and collection of federal income taxes. The IRS prints and distributes tax forms and audits tax returns. It is part of the Department of the Treasury.

Legal Lending Limits: statutory limit applied to banks/ financial institutions regarding loans made to a single entity. This amount is a function of stockholder equity.

Leveraged COLI (Leveraged Corporate Owned Life Insurance): the policyholder borrows against the cash value of the policy.

M & E Charge: the mortality and expense charge paid to the issuing carrier which includes the non-investment cost of an insurance contract.

MEC (Modified Endowment Contract): a type of contract that meets the requirements of Code section 7702, was entered into on or after June 21, 1988, and fails to meet the seven-pay test. Distributions from MECs are subject to taxation rules that differ from the rules governing the taxation of distributions from life insurance policies that are not MECs. Note that most BOLI transactions are MECs.

Mortality Charge: the pure cost of life insurance death benefit within a policy. It represents a cost to the purchaser and an income item to the carrier. Mortality charges retained by the carrier are used to pay claims.

Mutual Insurance Company: company owned by its policyowners; no stock is available for purchase on the stock exchanges.

NASD (National Association of Securities Dealers): organization of brokers and securities dealers in the over-the-counter (OTC) market operation under the auspices of the Securities and Exchange Commission (SEC). Its purpose is to enforce, on a self-regulation basis, the rules of the SEC, which are designated to protect investors against fraud and market manipulation of stocks. Insurance agents selling variable life insurance, variable annuities and mutual funds are required to be licensed by the NASD.

Net Coverage Amount: is the dollar face amount of death benefit amount of the life insurance policy less any outstanding loans or interest expense.

Non-forfeiture Values: are benefits of an individual whole life insurance policy that cannot be given up by the carrier. The policyowner has the right to choose from four different options: (1) to relinquish the policy for its cash surrender value; (2) to take reduced paid-up insurance;

(3) to take extended term insurance; (4) to use the loan value to borrow against the policy.

Non-MEC: an insurance contract that is not a Modified Endowment Contract. It is any insurance contract where the majority of premiums are made after the first of 3 years.

Nonqualified: benefit plans that are not approved by the IRS for tax breaks and which do not have to follow ERISA regulations. With a nonqualified plan, the same benefit plans do not have to be offered to all employees; employees can be chosen by the corporation depending upon whom it wants to give the benefit to. An example would be a nonqualified deferred income plan.

Non-accredited Investor: is an investor not meeting the net worth requirements of Regulation D. Nonaccredited investors are counted for purposes of the 35-investor limitation under Rules 505 and 506 of Regulation D.

OCC (Office of the Comptroller of the Currency): was created as a result of the National Currency Act of 1863 and the National Banking Act of 1964. The OCC is the prime regulator for all U.S. nationally chartered banks and is the organization that performs examinations and rulings on the national banks.

OTS (Office of Thrift Supervision): was created by Congress in 1989 to assume most of the regulatory and supervisory powers of the Federal Home Loan Bank Board, which Congress disbanded that year. The OTS charters federal savings and loan associations and federal savings banks. However, these institutions are examined by the FDIC, which administers the insurance fund for S&Ls. The OTS is responsible for issuing regulations that govern the activities of S&Ls and S&L holding companies.

Paid-up Insurance: life insurance policy under which all premiums have already been paid, with no further premium payment due, such as limited or single payment life insurance policy.

Participation Rate: the yield on the PEP life insurance product that is based upon a certain amount of investment participation in the S&P 500 index. This rate will lie somewhere between the guaranteed floor rate and the maximum ceiling rate of the product.

Pecuniary: consisting of money, that which can be valued in money. A pecuniary loss is a loss of money or one that can be translated in terms of money.

Pension Plan (Benefits): retirement program to provide employees (and often spouses) with a monthly income payment for the rest of their lives. To qualify, an employee must have met minimum age and service requirements. Benefit formulas can be either the defined contribution pension (money purchase plan) or the defined-benefit plan. The Employee Retirement Security Act of 1974 (ERISA) requires a pension plan to provide an income for the rest of a retired employee's life, and at least 50% of that amount to the surviving spouse of a retired employee for the rest of his/her life, unless the spouse waives this right in writing. Death and disability benefits are also provided by most pension plans. The Tax Reform Act of 1986 has changed the vesting requirements. Funds for these plans can be generated under numerous pension plan funding instruments.

Policy Date (Effective Date): date on which an insurance policy goes into force.

Policy Loan: In life insurance, a loan can be taken against the cash value of a life insurance policy at any time. The policyholder does not have to repay the loan until the policy matures or until the loan and any outstanding interest equals the cash value.

Policy Reserve (Prospective Reserve): amount designated as a future liability for life or health insurance to meet the difference between future benefits and future premiums.

Premium: the rate that an insured is charged, reflecting his or her expectation of loss or risk. The insurance company will assume the risks of the insured in exchange for a premium payment. Premiums are calculated by combining expectation of loss and expense and profit loading.

Private Placement: is a technique used by insurance companies in the purchasing of debt obligations of corporations as a means to: (1) void the uncertainties of the market; (2) replace market negotiations with private negotiations; and (3) avoid SEC restrictions. (I-p.373) It is an offering that complies with Regulation D (Rule 505 and 506); generally speaking, the offer of an unregistered security to no more than 35 non-accredited investors or to an unlimited number of accredited investors.

Proceeds: benefits payable under any insurance policy or annuity contract.

Qualified: such as a "qualified pension benefit plan" that has been approved for certain tax breaks and follows the stringent set of ERISA guidelines. With a qualified plan, the same benefits must be offered to all employees.

RAP (Regulatory Accounting Principles): are guidelines set by bank regulators, particularly the Federal Reserve and OCC regulators, that are different from GAAP principles. RAP principles place limits or requirements on certain balance sheet items that banks must adhere to. These principles do not affect BOLI transactions.

Registered Product: a security (including variable insurance products) must be registered just as sales representatives and broker-dealers must be registered before they can offer or sell a security in a state. Under the guidelines of the Uniform Securities Act, no person can offer to sell any security in a state lawfully unless the: (1) security is registered under the Uniform Securities Act; (2) security is designated by the act as exempt from registration requirement; or (3) transaction is designated by the act as exempt from registration requirement. If a security is not exempt from the registrations requirement, the security is called a *nonexempt security.*

Regulation D: the securities regulation that exempts small public offerings from registration (those valued at no more than $5 million worth of securities offered during a 12-month period).

Risk-Based Capital: is the definitional guideline for bank-held assets defined by the Federal Reserve, the OCC, and the FDIC. There are four classifications of bank assets calculated as a function of risk. The classifications begin with Tier 1 (least risky) through Tier 4 (most risky). Each tier is weighted based upon its riskiness so as to indicate on the bank's balance sheet how the assets are invested. See table in Appendix C.

SEC (Securities and Exchange Commission): Federal agency empowered to regulate and supervise the selling of securities, to prevent unfair practices on security exchanges and over-the-counter markets, and to maintain fair and orderly market for the investor.

Securities Act of 1933: landmark legislation passed by Congress providing the first regulation of the securities markets. The law, enforced by the Securities and Exchange Commission (SEC), requires registration of securities issues and disclosure of material information about the financial condition of the issuers. Variable annuity and variable life insurance policies have been determined to be securities under the terms of this law and are subject to regulation both by the SEC and by the state insurance departments.

Securities Exchange Act of 1934: was enacted after the Securities Act of 1933, which regulates the primary issuance of securities. The Act of 1934 regulates the secondary trading of securities. The intent of this act is to maintain a fair and orderly market for the investing public. It seeks to attain this goal by regulating the securities exchanges and the over-the-counter markets. Commonly called the Exchange Act, it formed the Securities Exchange Commission and gave the Commission authority to oversee the secondary markets and to register and regulate the exchanges. It requires several other entities to register with the SEC, including exchange members and broker-dealers who trade securities OTC and on exchanges and individuals who affect securities trades with the public.

Separate Account Products: life insurance products that are structured with carrier investments that are not found or held within the carrier's general account. They are variable rate products that have fluctuating yields based upon the investments within the separate account. Because this account is "separate" from the main, general account of the carrier, it reduces what is called carrier risk for the buyer's behalf.

Seven-Pay Test: applies to the test of a MEC. A policy will fail this test if the accumulated amount paid under the first 7 years exceeds the sum net level premiums (the MEC level)

Single Premium: one premium payment is made and the

policy is fully paid up with no further premiums required. Also, if all of the premiums are paid within 4 years from the date of purchase or on which an amount is deposited with the insurer for the future payment of premiums (of a substantial amount greater than 73 percent).

Split-Dollar Life Insurance: a type of plan that splits a life insurance policy's premium obligation and policy benefit between two individuals or entities, usually employer and employee. The two parties share the premium costs while the policy is in effect, pursuant to a prearranged agreement. At the death of the insured or the termination of the agreement, the parties split the policy benefits or proceeds in accordance with their agreement.

Stochastic: a statistical term which describes a variable with values determined by chance (a random variable). In regression analysis, the dependent variable is stochastic if the model does not perfectly explain all observations.

Stock Insurance Company: business owned by stockholders, as contrasted to a mutual insurance company, which is owned by its policyholders. Earnings of a stock insurance company are paid in shareholder dividends. Many major life insurers are mutual companies whereas some leading property/casualty and multi-line insurers are stock insurance companies.

Stockholders' Equity: is a balance sheet item that includes the book value of ownership in the corporation. It includes capital stock, paid-in surplus and retained earnings. It is equal to the total assets minus the total liabilities of a corporation. It is also known as net worth.

Universal Life Insurance: adjustable life insurance under which: (1) premiums are flexible, not fixed; (2) protection is adjustable, not fixed; and (3) insurance company expenses and other charges are specifically disclosed to a purchaser. This policy is referred to as unbundled life insurance because its three basic elements (investment earnings, pure cost of protection, and company expenses) are separately identified both in the policy and in the annual report to the policyowner.

Whole Life Insurance (Ordinary Life Insurance): policy that remains in full force and effect for life of the insured, with premium payments being made for the same period.

Withdrawal (Cash Withdrawal): removal of money from an individual life insurance policy or an employee benefit plan. A cash withdrawal from a life insurance policy reduces the death benefit by the amount of the withdrawal plus interest thereon. When a cash withdrawal is made from an employee benefit such as a pension plan, the employee usually forfeits all benefits purchased on the employee's behalf by the employer.

Yield: the rate of return on an investment.

BIBLIOGRAPHY

Dictionary of Business Terms, 3rd Edition, Barron's Educational Series, Inc., Hauppauge, NY, 2000

Dictionary of Insurance Terms, 4th Edition, Barron's Educational Series, Inc., Hauppauge, NY, 2000

Money & Banking, 5th Edition, American Bankers Association, Washington, D.C., 2003

McGill's Life Insurance, 5th Edition, Edward E. Graves, The American College, Bryn Mawr, Pennsylvania, 2004

Tax Facts on Insurance & Employee Benefits, 2006 Edition, The National Underwriter Company, Cincinnati, OH

ADDITIONAL THOUGHTS

The American College is pleased to present this book by Tom Wamberg, CLU, to the financial services community. For many years employee benefit programs for executives of corporations large and small have been financed through corporate-owned life insurance. This book uncovers a major aspect of this market, bank-owned life insurance, with clear and thorough explanations of the concept in practice. We think the book will be helpful to practitioners working in this and related areas of financial practice.

The American College does not endorse nor recommend specific financial planning concepts as solutions to specific problems, but we think it is helpful to bring well-thought-out ideas to the community for their information and consideration. Similarly, we do not by publishing this book intend to provide tax or other legal advice. Each client should consult his or her own advisors.

John J. McFadden, JD
Robert K. Clark Chair in Executive Compensation and Benefit Planning
Professor of Taxation and Pensions
The American College